It's Not Abou...

*To all who have suffered and
will suffer from the failure of humanity.*

For Doug and Denise

Comments From Readers

"**When I started to read this book I didn't know Richard Ingelido. When I finished I felt I had known you all my life. This book held me from beginning to end.** This story is full of struggle, grief and amusement, which any family will relate to during "Nam"; the young fathers who went and came back strangers. I'm so pleased that your life has had a peaceful and happy ending.

On a final note, you have achieved what every writer would like to hear, **I want to read this book again. Well done.**"

Kind regards, Penny Cooper

"**As an active anti-war protester during the Vietnam War, I only heard one side of the story.** Even though I still believe the war was wrong, I realized the damage we'd done to the many men and women who fought because going to war for your country was the thing that seemed right to do.

It was fascinating to read the day-to-day struggles from such a unique perspective. Richard tells a tale that makes the happenings vivid so many years later. Richard was not a soldier (but he lived at close range) and that gave him an interesting vantage point.

It was also a wonderful opportunity to see into my cousin, Richard's life and get to know how he became the loving, open-minded, compassionate man he is today."

Nancy A. Petenbrink, PhD

"I have read several books on the Vietnam conflict, although most have been from either a military or political perspective. This is the first account I have read of the experiences of a civilian contractor in a war zone.

When I picked up the book I had no expectations other than curiosity. I found however that **I was gripped by the reality and had to read it through before putting it down. I found the writing style refreshing and personal, and felt as if Dick was narrating the words himself.**

Dick has obviously faced some major issues in his life, conquered them and has become one of the most charming people I have met. This book is a great legacy".

Stuart Corbett

Order Book/s by email: <u>NotAboutWar@yahoo.com</u>

Ingelido, Richard 1940-

It's Not About the War

Author: Richard "Dick" Ingelido

Photographer: Richard Ingelido   Camera: Minolta SLR 35mm

With exception, photos of author: (unknown photographer/s)

Book Cover and Arts Design: Richard Ingelido

Cover Feature: Vietnamese papa san just finished praying in church.

Editor and Final Proof Reader: Dr. Nancy A. Petenbrink, Ph.D

ISBN: 0-646-45441-2

First printed in 2005 by Queensland Complete Printing Services Nambour, Qld. Australia

Disclaimer: All details given in this publication are true and correct to the best of my knowledge. Care has been taken in the research of the information herein, but no responsibility can be accepted by the author for any damages resulting from the information of this work.

<u>Special thanks to:</u>

Mother (Ellen Meyer) for the amazing love and trust only a mother can give.

Dr. Nancy A. Petenbink for all the time she has put into this book coupled with the encouragement she has given me. She is not only my cousin, but also a good friend.

Moya Pennell for her valuable input and enthusiasm.

There are too **many other people** to name and thank for their contribution of assistance and constructive criticism. You know who you are and I thank each and every one of you.

Last but not least I would like to thank my wife **Susan** for her assistance, years of understanding and devoted love.

Mass Through Time

Life is a formula of mass through time on roads fragile and uncertain;
calculating and reevaluating the transition from one heading to the other.
Peering over the horizon, for a glimpse of the future,
avoiding the obstacles while maneuvering from pillar to post..
We encounter a great deal of pushing and shoving in route,
all the while seeking in our minds, how we can gain the most.

Life is the old and the new.
The values change with review.
What was important is no longer.
In age we hope to become stronger.
Not just in body, but your mind to nurture.
Searching the past to improve your future.
But needs are different yet some the same.
In survival, we play these little mind games,
and then after dispute we have only ourselves to blame.

So-called set-backs come in cycles, it seems.
The sand blows and then be-calmed,
but inclement weather is always near.
The only advise to be given is to
ride the waves, set your sails,
and enjoy the transition,
with little affliction.

And when it's over you will realize,
storms move you much further ahead from where you would have been.
So goes the movement of mass though time.

Richard Ingelido

Contents

It's Not About The War

INTRODUCTION

This is a story in part about my unforgettable experience in Vietnam and how it affected my life. It is intended to reflect my own perspective and is an actual account of my experiences. *To the best of my ability, all the events and locations in this book are factual; but the exact date or sequence of events may not be entirely correct. Some names have been changed to protect the individual or their families.*

This book is in some ways chapters of " short stories" pieced together about my experience in Vietnam that will offer the reader a "broad and detailed perspective" during that period.

Before I tell you about my experience in Vietnam, it would be a good idea to give the reader a brief account of my background, qualifications and what I had to gain.

Please be aware that there is a Glossary of Terms on page 181.

I was born in a small, modest house in Everson, Pennsylvania on Jan 20, 1940. My sister Karen was born about five years later and became my father's "little girl." My mother seemed to be always defending me and trying to reduce the everyday beatings from my father. There was seldom enough money to pay the day-to-day bills and there were ongoing disturbing arguments between my mother and father after his return from his "secret rendezvous."

I was never much for indoor activities, especially school. The first couple of years in school were very difficult mostly because I was color blind and left handed. The teachers were appalling, treating me as though I had a learning disorder. The kids in my class would call me "dumb" because I couldn't "learn colors" and I seemed to be always getting into trouble with the teachers because I "didn't apply myself." On the other hand I was able to make friends easily and would always stand up for myself or for anyone that was getting pushed around by bullies. I had "fun" in school, but I fought my way through those years physically and mentally.

I loved the outdoors and belonged to the Boy Scouts for about five years. I excelled in scouting and was picked as the Senior Scout Leader of our Troop. I was over the moon when I was selected as one of four scouts in the state of Pennsylvania to participate in a U.S. Jamboree. I obtained a grade of Life Scout (One step below Eagle, the highest rank) and became determined to prove that I wasn't "dumb" as my classmates and father claimed. It gave me great satisfaction to finally prove to myself that I could be good at something that was of interest to me. I could always count on my mother to give me words of encouragement and to give me the freedom to do as I wished.

1

In the school vacation periods, I worked at whatever job I could get or do; from working on the rides with a traveling carnival at 15, to cleaning toilets in gasoline stations, unloading fruit crates, paper routes, setting duck pins in the bowling alley or making hay and cleaning the cow manure from the gutters on a dairy farm. I learned to cut men's hair when I was 13. His father trained my father and dad taught me the skill while cutting my friends hair over the years. It didn't matter what job I did as long as I could make a little cash and be somewhat independent.

By the time I was 15, I was almost making enough money to support myself, although it meant living in my great grandfather's chicken coop. The coop was not used for chickens anymore but for storage. I moved in after a dispute between my parents. I found it cold in the winter but there were very few choices at that time. It was a great feeling to be totally independent for the first time in my life. I later moved back to my parent's house to finish my last few months of 12th grade so my mother could help me study to get the grades I needed to graduate.

I graduated from Scottdale Joint High School in 1957, but was almost at the bottom of the class. I didn't care much and was happy enough to get the diploma. I knew it wasn't because I didn't have the intelligence to do better, but I didn't have the encouragement by the teaching staff or my father. My mother was the driving force that "pushed" me through school and encouraged me to finish. I longed for final freedom from the shackles of my father's cruelty and was ready to move to the next stage of my life.

About the same time I had found that my father had been supporting a mistress who had given birth to his child with another on the way. All the pieces fell into place for me and I felt a total loss of faith and respect for my father. I was shattered by the fact that I had existed in a lie all my life and yet my father would beat the hell out of me for telling lies. I was angry about the contradiction of values. My mother had known about his lies and other life for some time, but kept it from me. Mother's reasoning was that she wanted Karen and I to grow up and have a father.

At that time no decent paying jobs and seemingly no prospects were available in Southwestern Pennsylvania other than working in glass factories, steel mills or coalmines. Even those jobs were almost impossible to get. I couldn't afford to further my education and didn't believe I could pass the entrance exams, even if I had the finances.

Now 17, I decided to sign up for the U.S. Marines maybe in hindsight to prove to my father that I could make it in one of the toughest divisions of the military forces. I had always loved airplanes and could only dream of working in aviation. I enlisted for 3 years and found while in boot camp that I would not be accepted in the Marine Air Wing as promised by the recruitment officer before joining. I tore a cartilage in my right knee on an obstacle course that lead to ongoing problems. With that and a "cut-back" in government funding for the Marines, I was offered an Honorable Discharge after only six months of duty. I jumped at the chance as I could see I was not going to get what I wanted even if I stayed in for the required three years.

Shortly after my discharge from the Marines in December 1957, my dad, who was a foreman with a steel construction company, surprised me by arranging an interview. I was hired as a laborer, making $1.65 per hour.

I dated a few girls over the next couple of months before I met Doris Porter. Doris was an identical twin from a poor family and had five other siblings. She was very anxious to leave home and raise a family of her own. We fell in love and within six months we married. Doris was 16 and I was a few months short of 19. At the time it was not unusual to be married at such a young age. Nine months later on July 25, 1959 we had our first child, Donna. I wasn't happy having a child so soon, but after she arrived I was not sorry. She was, it seemed like, a living doll, with all the blond curls to match. I cannot express the love I felt for her.

Within two years, I had worked my way from a laborer to a "hangar" or steel erector. At first I didn't work for my Dad, but with other foremen. They could see that I was eager to learn and gave me plenty of lead to do so. I did all the high and difficult, steel erection, smoke stack repairing, and steeplejack work. My life was going well and I was soon making $3.65 per hour!

By this time my father heard from the other foremen that I was progressing well. My Dad and I finally started to warm up to each other and it was great to see another side of him that I didn't know existed.

All the work was very dangerous but I found it thrilling and challenging like nothing I had ever experienced. I had numerous narrow escapes that were life threatening to say the least, but managed to escape without injury until an early winter's day in 1960 my number came up.

We were short of men that day and I was assisting the ground crew. We were erecting a conveyor that would carry coal to a storage silo. I was directly beneath a 40-foot, 3,000 lb conveyor section, holding a single guideline tied to one end of it. The crane was lifting the section into the hands of an erector located about 100 feet in the air. As soon as my "buddy erector" was able to get his hands on one end of the conveyor, I was to climb the beamed structure to "spud" the other end in place. But as the section reached about 35 to 40 feet in the air, the clutch failed on the crane winch and the load fell without warning. I was standing directly under it and when the guideline I was holding went slack, I realized I was in trouble. I turned, hunched over in an attempt to jump clear, but the impact of the conveyor drove me to the ground.

My body felt completely numb and I was aware of having difficulty breathing. I was lying on my stomach unable to move but, through a small opening, I could see men's shoes kicking dirt and I could hear frantic yelling,

"Get this off him". Finally the opening widened and I could see light. Men bursting with adrenaline were straining above me as they lay the mass of steel to one side.

After more than an hour, an ambulance arrived at the site. By this time my body was in unbearable and indescribable pain and I had no feeling in my legs. The three-mile ride on the deeply rutted dirt track, before the main road to the hospital, was the most grueling undertaking I would ever experience.

I was not quite 21, married with a child and suffering from a crushed and dislocated 3rd lumbar vertebra. I also sustained numerous broken ribs (sheared off at the spine), partial paralysis in my right leg, a dislocated right shoulder and internal injuries. I was on my back for a couple of weeks, my spine stretching in an "A" frame position with weights hanging from my head at one end and from my legs at the other. It was an attempt to realign my 3rd lumbar and avoid a major operation. Thankfully it worked. After the feeling returned to my legs a plaster of paris cast was applied from my neck to my pubic bone. After 3 months the cast was removed and for the next 9 months I wore a lightweight alloy brace to keep me from bending at the waist. I was extremely lucky to survive such a horrific accident and not end up totally disabled.

For years following the accident I experienced terrifying nightmares. I had frequent dreams of being crushed in automobile or other accidents. The pain was re-lived over and over. I would wake in a cold sweat, with my heart pounding excessively and fighting for breath.

The $35 a week that I received from workman's compensation didn't go very far towards feeding a family for the two years of my recovery. To supplement my income, I sold honey from my beehives, planted a vegetable garden and cut hair for .50 cents a head. Fortunately we were eligible to purchase Government Food Stamps and that greatly reduced the cost of our food each week.

The Doctors informed me that I would never be able to return to work as an "Iron Worker" or any other position that required heavy lifting. Under those circumstances I qualified for a Pennsylvania State Rehabilitation Program. I initially decided to train as a barber but after I took my interest and qualifying exams for the program, I was informed that I had a broader range of choices. I found I could attend a college and get into aviation, if I passed the entrance exams. This was my big chance to realize my dream. Financially I had to get back to work quickly and opted for two years of college (14 months, full time, without a summer break) instead of four years for a full degree.

I went to night school for a couple of months and crammed for the entrance exams for Pittsburgh Institute of Aeronautics. I didn't do well in the exam, but I passed! I felt right at home with my courses and did well because I was one of the older and more adjusted students. An added incentive to achieve was the birth of my son Douglas on June 16, 1962. During college I continued to cut fellow student's hair and worked on weekends at Scottdale / Mount Pleasant Airport as an aircraft mechanic. Working at the airport gave me the chance to learn to fly at a greatly reduced price. I managed to solo and get my Student License after about 15 hrs of flying an Aeronca 7AC (fabric, single engine, tail wheel). I couldn't afford the time or money to obtain my Private License then, but did so later after my return from Vietnam. I graduated from the Institute in the top 5% of my class.

After graduation on March 22, 1963, aged 23, Avco Lycoming in Stratford, Connecticut offered me a position. I was hired and classified as an Experimental Assembly Technician working in Research and Development of gas turbine engines. I felt that it was a chance in a lifetime as very few people knew much about gas turbines and even less had a background with them. Avco Lycoming provided the T-53 turbine engines for the Bell helicopters "Hueys" that were used extensively in Vietnam.

The following year on July 15, 1964 my youngest daughter, Denise, was born. She was perfect in every way. I was thrilled to hold her and she added an overwhelming joy to my life. Now 24 with a wife and three children, it was all happening too fast for my pocket book to catch up! Somehow I needed to advance and increase my income.

After two years in experimental, I had a chance to advance within Avco. A junior engineering position became vacant and I was accepted, but my current supervisor would not approve my transfer because I was an asset to his department. I tried again, this time by applying for a job in Field Service Engineering. They were desperate for qualified and experienced people to go to Vietnam. I was accepted, but again thwarted by my supervisor.

I wanted to better myself but was held back on every move. I was frustrated and wondering what my next move was going to be when the local Metropolitan Life Insurance Agent came to my house to collect the monthly premium. He offered me a job as an agent. This was making a 90-degree turn from the direction I was on, but Mr. Nolan made it sound like I would be successful in selling insurance and make a very good living at it. "With your ambitions the sky is the limit", he said. I asked myself, "What did I have to lose?" I was offered a guaranteed salary of $100 a week for the first six months until my commissions "kicked-in", potentially making a lot of money! My area ("book") would be Ansonia, Connecticut so even a move from our rented apartment wasn't required.

I resigned from Avco and two weeks later was off to New York City to do my Met.Life training course and learn all the in applicable rules and regulations. I was required to pass a three-part Connecticut State License Examination to become a qualified insurance agent. I was informed before I took the exams that less than 50% passed on the first attempt, but I passed the

5

first time with high marks. Again I proved to myself that if I applied myself, I could succeed.

On the other hand, I found very quickly that I was not a "sales person" and felt uncomfortable trying to sell something that many families could not afford. By the end of three months I could see that I was not going to be "rolling in money", as first thought. In fact, I was not even going to earn enough to make a living.

I saw an advertisement in the local paper that Sikorsky, in Stratford, Connecticut, was looking for an Aircraft Mechanic (A&P) to work in the experimental flight hangar on the prototype CH53 helicopter. I applied for the position and was hired to work on the second shift from 4 pm to 12 am.

I informed my supervisor, Mr. Nolan, that I was leaving Metropolitan Life and he was shocked. He was already carrying two other vacant positions and collecting those "books." Mr. Nolan explained that he was very understaffed and unable to hire new agents. In desperation he proposed that I continue to collect my "book" with no requirement to sell new policies, until he found someone to fill my slot. I agreed to this and continued to collect premiums during the day and work the second shift at Sikorsky.

Until this point in my life I was never able to save any money and lived from paycheck to paycheck, so this opportunity to save and buy our first home was heaven sent. I worked the two jobs for about three months and was able to save $600 for a down payment towards a $12,000 house on Naugatuck Mountain, Connecticut. The two-bedroom house with a single bathroom was small for a family of five, but it was on three-quarters of an acre so the kids had a plenty of outside space to play and we all loved the isolation of the country.

After working in the experimental flight hangar at Sikorsky for a year, I became aware of a position at Avco Lycoming for a Technical Training Instructor. Now 26, I finally realized that turbine engines were my greatest interest and the knowledge I had gained about them became my greatest strength. My application was successful and I completed a three-month training program to become a qualified Instructor. I then taught ten, three-week military courses and numerous commercial classes on the T53-L13 engine. I was responsible for conducting formal classes to upgrade the training of all the Avco Technical Representatives. After two years of working in the training department, I was known by my colleagues and students as "Boy Instructor"; but was well respected as an authority on the engines.

As a young man of 28 I was struggling with internal conflict, trying desperately to decide what my "personal legend" (Taken from the book, The Alchemist by Paulo Coelho) should be. I enjoyed my position but I was starting to feel confined and wanted to move on to better and more exciting things.

I became aware of positions available at AiResearch Manufacturing Company (Garrett) in Phoenix, Arizona. The single opening that caught my eye

6

was a Special Military Contract to cover the newly designed and manufactured T76 engine installed on the North American Aviation, OV-10 "Bronco."

One of the prerequisites was to have a Secret Security Clearance. Such a clearance had been issued to me while working at Avco Lycoming and it was easily transferable. I couldn't help but jump at the chance and after an extensive screening process, was welcomed with open arms.

After joining Garrett in the early months of 1968 I was given three months of technical training at Phoenix then sent to my first assignment at North American Aviation in Columbus, Ohio. Although the Marine and Air Force OV-10's had been in production at that location for some time, they had recently began the process of delivering them. It was a beehive of activity and the new engine installation had a number of unique problems.

After three months at North American, I was given a Military Contract for two months at the Naval Air Test Center in Pax River, Maryland. I provided technical for the T76 engines during the final OV-10 acceptance flights and aircraft carrier trials. The next step was to pack my bags for the USMC base, Camp Pendleton in California to prepare for my Special Assignment in Nam.

I went to Vietnam as a non-combatant and was treated differently by the U.S. Military and Vietnamese alike. The men and women in the U.S. military were so close to their individual tasks, it made it difficult for them to see the big picture. They had a job to do and orders to follow. I was fortunate enough to be autonomous; consequently, I experienced a broader picture of what occurred. I was able to get closer to the local Vietnamese civilians to see how they survived in their war-ravaged country.

As a civilian, I was issued a "Special Assignment" by the U.S. Government to support the 1st Marine Air Wing OV-10 reconnance aircraft. My assignment would take me within a couple miles of the Demilitarized Zone (DMZ). I had *total freedom of travel* in or out of the country, whenever I deemed necessary. The assignment was far beyond just keeping aircraft in the air. It was also a fact-finding mission on the status of engine utilization and assist in aircraft positioning. I was to observe, first hand, the condition of the aircraft/engines and report my findings back to the 1st Marine Air Wing Headquarters. I was required to send engineering status reports to AiResearch, the manufacture of the T76 engines, to assist in redesigning the engine and improve reliability.

The task I was undertaking would change my life and my family relationship in more ways than I was able to recognize at the time. I thought I was doing my country a service and making money for my future. Life was full of uncertainties before my experience and it became more emotionally charged and challenging as time went on. The years of 1968 and 1969 were a shock wave of change with an eruption of human emotions for my family, the world and me.

Map of Vietnam and Surrounding Countries

Marble Mt. Air Field: Located at S.E. tip of Da Nang aircraft's right-wing

Map from Da Nang to DMZ

Map of MMAF

Marble Mountain and Air Field

MMAF Looking North. Note Highway 1 on the left side running top to bottom.

Below: Note the of lack of plant life due to spraying agent orange around the mountains. Highway 1 is running north/south in the center of photo.

OV-10:

OV-10 Line Drawing

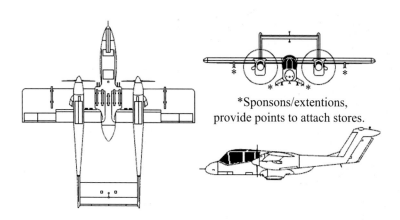

*Sponsons/extentions, provide points to attach stores.

Statistics of the OV-10:

Wing Span: 40 feet (12.2 meters)
Length: 41 feet, 7 inches (12.7 meters)
Height: 15 feet, 1 inch (4.6 meters)
Weight: 7,190 lbs. (3,261 kilograms)
Max Gross Take off Weight: 14,444 lbs. (6,552 kilograms)
Max Speed at Sea Level: 244 knots (452 kilometers/hr)
Service Ceiling: 28,800 feet (8,778 meters)
Crew: One pilot and one Arial Observer (AO)/ ordnance officer. (Removal rear seat for greater fuselage cargo capacity)
Fuel: 5 self-sealing fuel tanks in wing. 552 Gallons capacity (954 liters) 150, 230 or 300 Gallons (568, 871 or 1136 liters) external tank
Range: 700 nautical miles (2224 kilometers) with a 150 gal drop tank.

Mission Performance: 5.5 hrs loiter time with the 150 gal drop tank and 2 hrs loiter time with full ordnance load

Note: For more OV-10 detailed information, visit page 189 of this book.

USA Passport of Richard Ingelido Containing Department of State Stamp

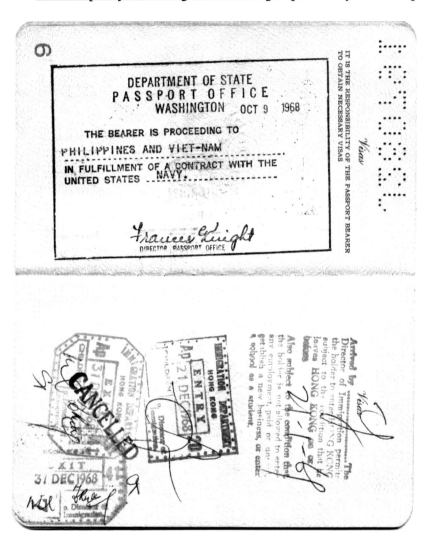

Chapter: 1
Getting There

I picked up my Orders from the U.S. Defense Department in Washington DC on October 9, 1968. My passport was stamped, "The Bearer is proceeding to Philippines and Vietnam in fulfillment of a contract with the United States Navy." My "AVO" (Avoid Verbal Orders) was a "Special Assignment with the U.S. Marine Corps." The upper echelon of the Marines fell under the jurisdiction of the U.S. Navy Department even though they didn't like to admit to it! From Washington D.C., I went directly to Camp Pendleton Marine Base in California. I had a "two week crash course" to update my very rusty Paris Island Marine infantry training, latest weapons and military procedures prior to my departure with the 1st Marine Air Wing to Vietnam.

I noticed during the training session that the Marine Drill Instructors "DI's" didn't have much time for a civilian or "maggot" as I was addressed on most occasions. To them, I was "lower than whale shit on the bottom of the ocean". Most Marine "DI's" detest weakness and consider civilians as "bottom feeders".

Flying Tiger Airlines was under a contract with the U.S. Government to fly military personnel from the U.S. to Vietnam. The airlifts were commonly known as MACV (mac vee) flights and stretched DC-8 aircraft were used. After my two week survival and orientation course, I departed Camp Pendleton on November 2, 1968 on one of these flights.

As I was waiting to board the late evening flight I tried to remember the faces of my family. I hadn't seen them for almost a month. I felt confused and tried desperately to understand how I had come to be in this situation. Then my thoughts wondered to my kids.

They were probably in their warm beds, in Pennsylvania. I started to reminisce about the end of the summer of 1968, my wife, Doris had moved back to her hometown of Connellsville, Pennsylvania and enrolled our three children in school. Her parents, twin sister, other sisters and brothers still lived there. They were a close-knit family and would be a support network for her while I was in Vietnam. I was glad to see it in one way, but I knew Doris would get some strange ideas from her old fashioned mother. Helen had tried to run our lives early in our marriage and it was difficult for me to get it turned around. Helen never had a job outside the house but raised six children. She believed a woman's place was in the home and a husband should be the sole income earner. Helen had the final say in household matters and encouraged her children to carry on with her beliefs. This caused a great deal of friction at the time and uncertainty about the future of my marriage.

Reality returned to me when my name was called for boarding. I was one of two civilians on board and suddenly felt like I was stepping into another stage of my life. I felt lonely and unsure about what my future was going to bring. Although 28 years old, I felt much older and I was a little uneasy in the company of all the young Marines, known as hard core "grunts." Most of the Marines seemed to be in their late teens and early twenties. They looked very confident with their muscular bodies and close shaved heads.

Grunt is a chivalrous term used to describe a ground-pounding (infantry) Marine. I use it with respect. Within the Marine Corp. ranks, the infantry was also known as "The Crotch." These men fought on the front lines face to face with the enemy. Only they really knew what the war was like on the front line. Most of them were not able to tell their stories and only faced the horror in recurring nightmares.

By the time I boarded the aircraft it looked like a half loaded cargo bay. The grunts had all their gear in the main cabin and it appeared to me they could hit the deck running as soon as the main gear touched down in Vietnam. The Marines were burdened with backpacks, sea bags, ammo belts, M-16s and handguns in holsters. Gear was everywhere, with overhead lockers and areas under the seats packed tightly, this made moving though the aisle nearly impossible. My assigned seat was already stacked with someone else's gear, so I pushed it into the over-cluttered aisle and slid into my cramped aisle seat. The seats were typical coach class standard with little legroom and cashes under foot. Some of the grunts were actually sitting on their gear because there was nowhere to put it. I couldn't imagine what was in the cargo holds, because it looked like everything was in the cabin! Furthermore, I had no idea how overweight/gross the aircraft was and I doubt that the pilot did either.

I assumed most of the Marines knew nothing about the theory of flight. An "over gross situation" to them was probably thought by most to be with a fat, ugly prostitute. Most appeared bored, but I'm sure there were some who were uptight. Me, I was just taking one step at a time. The first thing I was determined to do was survive the flight to Vietnam.

We departed from Southern California late at night as the cold night air provided greater air density for better engine performance and better lift off capabilities for our first leg to Anchorage, Alaska. The aircraft would arrive in Anchorage in the early hours of the morning and depart in the cold darkness of that same morning, this time bound for Japan.

The aircraft managed to get off the ground after an unusually long take off roll. No one else seemed to notice and most of the grunts were asleep shortly after take off. I sat in my seat, as uncomfortable as it was, smiled and nodded my head. I was able to feel a warped sense of humor in all this as though I was part of a black-comedy movie.

After a 2,425-mile flight leg we landed at Anchorage a few hours before daylight. I could see a light snow blowing across the landing lights and residual piles of snow on the ground. No one was allowed to disembark while the aircraft was being refueled. It was just a quick turnaround and ready to go again.

Suddenly, I was really concerned. We had to take on a lot more fuel for the leg to Okinawa, Japan than we needed from Pendleton to Anchorage. This next leg was going to be 3,700 miles. With the additional weight of the fuel we needed all the help of the cold morning and then some, to get in the air. I didn't know how much runway we had, but most major airports had at least 10,000 feet. Whatever the length, I was unsure if it would be enough. I kept reminding myself that flights such as this departed many times before and the pilots knew what they were doing. On the other hand, maybe they stretched the envelope a little too far this time.

During taxi out to the active runway, most of the grunts were already sound asleep. Once lined up on the active, the pilots locked the brakes and slowly advanced the power levers. The aircraft started to vibrate and the shaking increased as the engines accelerated toward takeoff power. Eventually the brakes could not hold the aircraft in position any longer and the take-off roll began as the pilots released the brakes.

The roll was very slow and it seemed to take forever to build up ground speed. I kept straining to see out the windows, trying to judge our ground speed in the darkness of the morning. All I could see were lights in the distance and found it impossible to judge. One thing for sure, it was taking an extremely long time and we had to be eating up one hell of a lot of runway.

Now the interior overhead panels were shaking so badly that one of the unsecured overhead lockers came open and gear tumbled out. A couple of Marines jumped from their seats, gathered the items and closed the door again.

They didn't seem to be disturbed that we still hadn't left the ground. My eyes focused back to the window on the reference lights in the distance and I wondered how much runway was remaining and if there were any obstacles at the end of it. I held my breath, waiting to run off the end of the runway and crash in a huge ball of flames.

I couldn't believe how slow our ground speed was when the pilot started pulling the nose up for takeoff. After a few seconds, what seemed like hours, I felt the wheels come off the hard-surface.

This was the flattest takeoff with the slowest climb rate I had ever experienced in an aircraft this size. We continued to lumber straight ahead and slowly gain altitude. It was precisely at that time I was ready to visit the toilet to check my underwear, but I suspected the pilots might already be there.

I was amazed to realize that most of the grunts were asleep one minute later. The cabin lights were turned off and I sat in the dark wondering what else might be in store for me over the next six months. It was impossible to ignore the pungent smell of male bodies filling the cabin. I knew that mine smelled no better and I had a long way to go before my next shower.

The leg to Okinawa was uneventful. I remember seeing Mt. Fuji on the right side of the aircraft a short time before our descent to Kadina Air Force Base in Okinawa. Again we were confined to the aircraft after our landing at Kadina. We were refueled and serviced; the toilets were purged and more cold sandwiches were loaded for the next leg. The final leg of our flight was to be 2600 miles before landing at Da Nang Main Air Base in Vietnam.

During my flight I spent the passing hours thinking about how and why I was on this aircraft going to a war. Before my departure to Vietnam there were many visions in my mind fuelled by the relentless media propaganda. Yet, one never knows exactly what anything is like until it is experienced. I really believed in the fight against communism and the fight for world freedom. Freedom to make ones own choices; everyone should have that right! I also believed that the South Vietnamese wanted democracy but the North wouldn't have it.

History told me that the U.S. was involved with Vietnam during World War II. The revolutionary leader Ho Chi Minh worked with the U.S. Office of Strategic Services (OSS) to pass information about Japanese troop movements in the area and had been instrumental in returning downed American pilots to the safety of China. In return, OSS provided small unit tactics and weaponry training to Minh's newly formed military group. However, after World War II, the U.S. began helping France in its efforts to reestablish colonial dominance in Vietnam and prevent communism from spreading into the remainder of South East Asia.

Then war broke out between the Ho Chi Minh regime and the French as Minh wanted to be free of the French. The U.S. began training French troops and pilots and operating cargo aircraft to support the French. Hanoi agreed to divide the country in half and a "Cease Fire Line" (DMZ) was established on July 22, 1954. The agreement started to unravel shortly after President Eisenhower declared that he would back the French with money, but not U.S. personnel. A few months later in October, Eisenhower pledged support to Ngo Dinh Diem, the head of the South Vietnam government. Eisenhower broke with the French to favor the establishment and aid in the development of South Vietnam as an independent nation, run by nationalists strong enough to resist the Communist invaders from Hanoi. This basic contradiction led to the displacement in 1955-56 of the French in the region by the U.S., which the French bitterly resented. To European countries, the U.S. action was not acceptable and then remained unwilling to support the U.S. in Vietnam throughout the war.

President John F. Kennedy felt very strongly about supporting South Vietnam and considered the situation as potentially having "A Domino Effect." Communism should be stopped here, or the remainder of Asia could fall. The U.S. stayed on to support the new alleged South Vietnam "Puppet" Government. In Aug 1964, the North began allegedly attacking U.S. Naval Ships in the Gulf of Ton Kin and infiltrating the South, causing mayhem. The hostility and conflict between the North and South increased each year. Aggression from the North threatened to overwhelm the South. President Johnson, backed by the Secretary of Defense Robert McNamara, believed an increase military presence was justified. "Police Action" seemed to be the tactic or policy best used by the U.S. to support South Vietnam. The U.S. policy was not to "invade" North Vietnam to win the war, but to defeat them by wearing them down. World opinion would not tolerate the U.S. so powerful with advanced high tech weapons, over running a third world country with no Air Force and very few weapons.

I thought I was going to be a freedom fighter, stop the "Domino Effect" and I had a good feeling about being a part of history. Not many people would get the opportunity to take part in action that might change the future of their descendants in a positive way. I could tell my children and grandchildren what "really happened." Also, it was an opportunity, I hoped, for me to make extra money for the future.

The involved dangers included in my assignment were unknown. When I worked for Avco Lycoming as a Technical Training Instructor, I trained almost all Lycoming Technical Representatives. They all had different stories to tell after their Vietnam assignment and gave me an idea about what I should expect. I was driven by the excitement and sense of adventure.

During military briefings, before I departed Camp Pendleton, I was warned of the dangers in Vietnam, like booby traps, prostitutes who would take you into the back room to waiting Viet Cong that would cut your throat and kids on the street begging for candy that may have been given a grenade with instructions to pull the pin when the time was "right." They went on to say that these warnings were usually indicative of the experience of individuals in different areas or environments. In other words, just because it can happen in one case or situation, it may not in another. A final word of caution was, "Don't trust any Gook or Slope Head; all the things we discussed happen on a regular basis, don't let it happen to you!"

Surprisingly we discussed not only the dangers I'd be confronting, but they also boasted of the good life the Vietnam experience could provide. Most of the men I spoke with, who had been stationed in the Saigon area, had a great time and wanted to return. Saigon was "Sin City" around the clock. Bars were open 24-hours while prostitutes, drugs and whatever your imagination could dream up was available.

The men in I Corp "up country" told a different story. A war was being fought. The bases were under attack and overrun periodically without warning. The living conditions were marginal to shithouse. Yet these men were much better off than a Grunt or GI who tried to survive fighting the ever elusive VC or "hard core" North Vietnamese (NVA).

Up country, there were no U.S. military passes given for the nearby towns. In fact, they were all listed as "off limits" and too dangerous. No good times were to be had for those looking for it. For them, the dream would be overseas leave in Hong Kong, Bangkok, Singapore, Manila and Sydney; a few of the favorites. Some actually went to Saigon for leave because it was cheap and had all the relief anyone could want. Most military assignments in Vietnam were for one year with R&R / I&I leave of 14 days given after six months of "in country" duty. Most of the men used it to get laid, lost in a bottle, or meet with wives or loved ones.

Chapter 2:
Arrival in Charlie's Country

I stepped off the stretched DC-8 aircraft after being confined for over 24 hours and immediately noticed an unfamiliar smell in the air. Smoke from cooking fires, food, spices, mold, animal and human defecation, integrated with the odor of perspiration, along with the high humidity were compressed into one pungent odor. I had never smelled anything like it before and unique to Asia.

The tarmac was steaming and still wet from a sudden shower. The humidity, even though it was only late morning, was stifling. While we were lined up on the hot blacktop waiting to be processed, I could feel perspiration running down the small of my back and felt it dripping from my eyebrows into my eyes. I thought nervously to myself, "If this is November what's it like in July?"

The constant roar of landing aircraft using reverse thrusting and departing aircraft using afterburners was deafening. No one in the line attempted to speak. Using afterburners, two F-4s caught my eye at take off, then climbed out at a steep angle of attack. They popped through a couple puffs of billowy clouds into the blue sky, then out of sight. I could almost cut the excitement with a knife.

Da Nang Main Airport was divided into two sections. Comparing the two was like night and day. The Air Force had various types of heavy fighter aircraft on one side of the runway protected by revetments. The Marine Air Wing on the other side had only helicopters of various shapes and sizes, also in revetments. The Air Force disliked the Marines for their "gung ho" attitude and the Marines defiantly expressed their attitude by giving their own special salute; a bastardized two finger "V" / peace sign. They would throw three fingers in the air with the "middle finger" between the "V" of the other two. Then defiantly say, "Fuck peace, war's our business!" The Marines wanted to win the war and get it over with.

On the other hand, due to better government funding, Marines resented the Air Force superior living conditions. The Air Force had air-conditioned, barracks or apartments with hot showers and mess the quality of a, four star buffet restaurant.

The Marines had "squat" by comparison. The living quarters, called "hooches", were about 18 by 35 feet and accommodated 6 to 8 men. The hooches were positioned in long rows and spaced about 10 to 15 feet apart. They were constructed of wooden frames covered with corrugated steel, or sometimes, plywood sheeting. For "air conditioning", the side walls had framed corrugated sheet windows, hinged to swing out/upward and could be propped open. The hooches had rough sawed wooden floors and sat on two-foot high stumps for ventilation. A hatch/door was located at each end of the hooch. On hot days, it was almost better to be outside in the sun than in one of those metal hot boxes. Sandbags and or empty wooden rocket boxes filled with sand were stacked closely around the hooches about 5 to 6 feet high to provide some protection from incoming mortars or rockets. Additional sandbags had to be spread out over the corrugated roofs to help hold the sheets in place during heavy windstorms.

****

My first stop "in country" was to report to Da Nang Main Air Base, 1st Marine Air Wing Headquarters. Every U.S. expatriate in Vietnam commonly referred to Vietnam as "in country." My orders were checked and I was briefed. I was to cover all of "I Corp" wherever there were OV-10s under the 1st Marine Air Wing (1st MAW). Within the 1st "Wing", my major responsibility was to support MAG-16 based at Marble Mountain Air Field, MAG-36 at Phu Bai, and MAG-39 at Quang Tri. Within the Marine Air Groups, were Squadrons of OV-10s designated as VMO. Marble Mountain Air Airfield (MMAF), or commonly known as "Marble", was to be my home base of operation. In all there were about 36 OV-10s; with about half positioned at Marble (VMO-2).

I was granted unrestricted travel and could authorize any investigation or necessary maintenance on Garrett T76 engines experiencing low power or premature failure. I was to participate in investigations of OV-10 crashes at the site if necessary, to determine whether enemy ground fire, pilot error, or engine related problems had caused the crash.

During my brief I was told about the military tender/monetary system used in Vietnam. Military Payment Currency, commonly known as "MPC" was used as legal tender on every military base to pay for all expenses. The MPC was paper only; no metal coins were used. U.S. dollars, commonly known as "green", were not to be used. In fact green were illegal to have unless you were departing the country on leave. Any green you had were required to be exchanged for MPC or transferred into a money order to send back to your bank or loved ones. No more than $200 MPC (enough cash for immediate needs) was permitted to be carried by any one person. Anything at the PX / BX that was needed over $200 could be purchased with a personal check or money order. The Vietnamese currency (Dong) was to be used off the base or for paying the local Vietnamese for goods and services.

The Golden Rule was not to exchange any money of any kind off base. I learned that this key rule and regulation was implemented to discourage people from exchanging money on the black market. On the black market (off base) you could get about two to three times the normal exchange rate using MPC to exchange for Dong. Green was highly prized by everyone and it had an exchange rate of four to six times the normal rate that was offered on the base.

Consequently Green traded in the black market would eventually trade its way to North Vietnam where the "hard cash" would buy gold or arms and equipment used for the North Vietnamese cause. Knowing that green ended up in the North was enough reason for me not to exchange money on the black market.

As an additional precaution against the black market, the U.S. Military would change the MPC giving only 24 hours notice that the current MPC would be null and void the following day. Each person on base had that day to exchange a maximum of $200 "old" MPC for the new. Those on leave out of country on R&R could exchange their MPC on the day of their return. This system left those who had more than their allowance, as well as the locals, with useless paper. The black market was limited in "I" sector, but in Saigon it thrived.

Exchange day was chaotic. Some tried to minimize their losses, while others tried to make a profit. If anyone had over the $200 permitted amount, they would search for someone who was under the $200 limit. The person under the limit would accept the excess at a 2 or 3 to one exchange rate. Final payment from the exchange "deal" was made when they received their new MPC. Locals working on the base might offer to sell their old MPC at 5 or 10 to one! It depended on how desperate they were. It was to your benefit to have only a few dollars MPC in your pocket when one of these reissues occurred. I saw one exchange of $2 green buy $200 of old MPC! One thing for sure, a hell of a lot of money changed hands on that day and not just at the Military Exchange Office.

Beyond the monetary system, I was warned not to wear any patches on my arms or have an I.D. badge on my chest because rumor was that a price of $25,000 was on the head of any American civilian or high-ranking officer. My capture was of particular concern because I had an overview of the total operation of the First Marine Air Wing. I was quietly handed a 45cal automatic pistol. I had qualified with a 45 as a young Marine more than 10 years before but hadn't touched one since. "How do you know I can use one?" I said to the young Captain. "Your orders say that you can", he replied with a straight face. Then with a crooked smile he said: "Keep the gun under your hat!" I didn't ask what he meant by that, but I assumed he meant that passing out handguns to civilians wasn't the normal thing to do. I was given my dog tags and non-combatant card. A non-combatant with a weapon! That made a hell of a lot of sense! Oh the irony. I figured if captured, I'd probably have my nuts cut off and stuffed in my mouth along with my non-combatant card.

After the briefing, I was assigned a bunk in a "transient" hooch for the night. I would be taken by truck to Marble Mountain Air Field the following morning. I was tired, hot, sweaty and weary since my last good sleep. The humidity and heat was oppressive and I was looking forward to a shower and a good stretch out in my bunk.

The public shower was constructed in the same way as the hooches; except the floor and drainage system consisted of loading skids (slatted wood) scattered around on top of the sand. Each shower building could accommodate about 30 to 40 men. We walked to and from the showers clad only in a towel, because there was nowhere to hang anything. Anything personal, other than that, would be stolen if it was placed on the outside wall of the shower building. Stealing seemed to be a way of life in the military.

At peak times in the evening and during heavy rains, the shower's drains could not accommodate the volume of water so the dirty water came up to our shins. The wooden skids floated around like rafts and were impossible to stand on. By the time I got back to my hooch I was covered with sweat again and had sand up to my ass from trudging through the soft sand in thongs. I decided not to wear thongs in the future when going for a shower.

At last, I collapsed into a "fart sack" (two sheets sewn together) on my bunk. It felt and smelled damp. I deduced I would have to adjust to sleeping in wet bedding, but I was overtired and unable to sleep in my new environment. The humidity was high with no air movement, but I finally fell asleep in my sweat soaked bedding while fending-off an onslaught of mosquitoes.

F-4 Take-off at Da Nang Main Airport

Chapter 3
Finding My Way Around

The 1st MAW, had received the OV-10 Broncos at Marble a couple of months before my arrival. Marble was the home of the OV-10 flight squadron VMO-2 (known as the angry two). The airfield was about seven miles southeast of Da Nang and the northern perimeter shared a common mile wide fence with a U.S. Army supply base. The eastern perimeter was located directly on a two-mile stretch of the South China Sea beach. It was covered with a maze of barbed and razor wire, machine gun bunkers and lookout towers.

At the southern perimeter, the Marine air base bordered a small Special Forces camp. About a mile from the south end of the base were five marble extrusions rising directly from the sand. These were the Marble Mountains. They ranged in height from about 100 to 500 ft. The highest and largest of the mountains was also the closest the southern perimeter. I was told that they were perforated with natural tunnels. Some were small and difficult to crawl through and others were room size caverns. It was later discovered that Charlie was using one of the larger caves as a hospital! They were right under our noses for years without our knowledge! Beyond the Marble Mountains to the south were rice paddies, water buffalo and thatched huts controlled by Charlie.

On the western perimeter was a two-mile stretch of fence, with a maze of razor wire and machine gun lookout posts. The 3rd Marines were headquartered and strategically positioned along this perimeter. Highway One bordered the western fence. Highway One began 125 miles northeast of Hanoi and terminates on the southern tip of Vietnam. At the time it was a two-lane road. The main base access gate was at the northern end of the western fence line and heavily fortified with bunkers and machine gun nests. Looking west in the distance, a clear view of "Charlie Ridge" could be seen across the rice paddies. The mountain ridge was approximately 20 miles south west of Da Nang and afforded the Viet Cong a route from Laos into the Da Nang area. The ridge was the site of many Marine operations aimed at disrupting Charlie's movement of men and supplies.

The most vulnerable spot of Marble was the western perimeter and the largest marble mountain directly south. On the other side of the west perimeter road was a "buffer zone." It was constantly defoliated with "agent orange." At night, flares lit up the western perimeter. If movement was detected, Spooky, known as "Puff" the Magic Dragon, was nearby to strafe the suspected area with ground fire. Puff was a C-47 (military version of a DC-3 aircraft) gunship with 3 mini gattling guns protruding through open fuselage windows on the left hand side of the aircraft. The mini guns were 7.62mm rounds and each gun was capable of firing 6,000 rounds a minute, for a total of 18,000 rounds per minute. Puff operated typically at 3,000 feet and 130 knots airspeed. With that kind of firepower, a round could be sprayed to the ground with about 12-inch spacing. One in every 5 rounds was a tracer, so the pilot could follow his rounds to the target. It was possible to sit at the back of our hooch at night and watch the steady stream of tracers from Puff to the ground. It looked like a small lava waterfall or a giant laser show put on for entertainment.

The main North/South runway, around 5,000 feet in length, was located close to the center of the base, our maintenance facilities and the aircraft revetments were located on the beach side or SE Corner. North of the maintenance facilities were the enlisted men's (EMs') hooches. The location of the living quarters were telling of rank, with the hooches of the enlisted men closest to the maintenance facilities and aircraft revetments; therefore closer to the danger of mortar and rocket attacks. The noncoms and the officers had hooches further north from the likely targets of the aircraft revetments area.

The 81 mm mortar only had a maximum range of 1.8 miles and could not reach the hooches, but the 122 or 140mm rockets launched by Charlie could easily reach 5 miles and inflict heavy casualties in every area of the base. The rocket attacks occurred randomly and usually in the middle of the night. The VC had a few hours of darkness to set up the rockets, place them on timers and be miles away when the rockets were fired. The rockets were originally designed to be fired from a launcher but the VC ingeniously fired them from earthen ramps using only sticks, mud and a battery timer to allow them time to escape.

****

I stayed in transient barracks until a bunk became available in a civilian hooch. When the first Rep was transferred to a stateside assignment, I planned to move to his spot in shared quarters.

My first priority was to visit three bases in the northern most part of South Vietnam, Hue/Phu Bai (MAG-36), Quang Tri (MAG-39) and the northern most airstrip, Dong Ha. The pressure was on me to slow down the premature-removal of OV-10, T76 engines. The engines seemed to be removed for little or no reason without proper trouble-shooting and The 1st Marine Air Wing had totally used up all their spare engines. In fact, many of the OV's were AOG (Aircraft On the Ground) due to no replacement engines available.

The Phu Bai base was located a few miles south of the city of Hue and close to the small province of Phu Bai. From Marble, it was almost due north approximately 65 miles and would be my first stop and visit.

With no guidelines in place I had to plan my own work schedule and make my own travel arrangements. I was told I could get on the daily manifest for the Marine C 130 flights, which departed from Da Nang Main Airport and made stops at Hue' and Quang Tri. The four-engine turboprop C-130s' carried cargo and or military personnel and flew at an altitude safe from the danger of ground fire. Although it was a safe way to travel it wasn't worth the hassle, because I would still have to make my own way from Marble Mountain to Da Nang Main.

Instead, I decided to depart directly from Marble on a transient helicopter. This was the option I chose for my first flight from Marble Mountain, not as safe but more direct.

I found the best way to get around up north was to wait at the helicopter re-fueling pad for a chopper going my way, show my badge, and jump on board. The choppers were usually Huey gunships, Huey slicks (without mounted machine guns), or Boeing CH-46 Sea Knights.

On that first day a Huey gunship with machine guns hanging from the rear doorways, made its approach and landed on the pad. The blasting sand from the rotor wash was stinging every exposed part of my skin. I turned my back to avoid the sand and dust storm till the Huey squatted on the skids and the pilot reduced collective pitch. I ran out while they were refueling the still running T-53-11 engine.

The two blades were rotating at a flat pitch, but with all the engine and gearbox noise, I found it difficult to talk with the pilot. I flashed my ID and asked where they were going. The pilot pulled out the chart (map) ran his finger from Marble Mountain, north to Hue. So I nodded my head and the pilot stuck his thumb out pointing to the back, indicating to climb aboard.

As I got in I noticed there were no seats or belts. I took a position behind the gunner's and sat on the floor. The gunners had helmets on with radio connections to the pilots, so at least for them it was quiet. There was no soundproofing insulation or doors in the ship so the whining noise of the engine and gearboxes was unbearable. I took a couple of 45cal bullets out of my pocket and stuck the round end of a bullet in each ear and could finally hear myself think.

The pilot pulled some collective to lift off, then pushed the nose forward with the cyclic to gain airspeed. I felt a sudden relief from the repressive humidity as the fresh air blew through the large door openings. Once underway, it was quite exhilarating. I had no idea of what lay ahead on this flight but for me, it was an exciting new experience.

We headed north across the flat landscape toward Da Nang Bay. I could see the occasional grass hut surrounded by rice paddies and workers in the fields. Water buffalo were pulling ploughs followed by ploughmen. I'd never seen anything like it before and felt overwhelmed. The scenery changed quickly as we passed over a heavy populated area. The pilot stayed at less than 100 feet above the ground for quite a while then started gaining altitude over Da Nang Bay to clear the line of mountains to the north. Hai Van Pass was a saddleback in the mountains and was used by helicopters to fly between the mountain peaks. As we cleared the saddle, we were only about 100 feet above ground again. At this altitude I had to hug myself to keep warm because of the cold air blasting through the open doors.

The view was spectacular. Directly below was a narrow twisting road leading through the pass with U.S. heavily fortified/armored bunkers strategically placed. Looking south, I could see the expanse of the bay, the sprawling city of Da Nang, Monkey Mountain Peninsula, and the white sands of China Beach stretching all the way to the Marble Mountains. Looking north, I could see the mountains descending to flat terrain and rice paddies spreading to the horizon. Looking east, the paddies turned into pristine white sandy beaches. The sheer beauty overcame me and for the moment I forgot the danger and tragic turmoil below.

Once we cleared the pass, we started our descent down the contour of the north side of the mountain range. As we started across the flats, I could see large craters in the ground. Everywhere the landscape was changed and made sinister by war. I could see reflections of the sun bouncing off the rain filled craters and realized there had been heavy bombing recently. The craters were so large, I wondered if any vegetation would ever grow there again. At the same time, I thought about the number of lives that had probably been lost in the area.

As we continued, now at tree top level and following the Perfume River, we were so low I could see local people going about their lives along the riverbanks. I thought, "What the hell are we doing so low?" Is the pilot trying to draw ground fire? I could sense the danger, but had no control. I decided to enjoy the ride and take a couple of pictures with my 35mm!

After landing at Phu Bai, I introduced myself at the MAG-36 Operations Desk and proceeded to find out how many AOG's or removed engines I had to deal with. At the end of the day I was assigned to a damp, smelly, transient hooch. I spent a long sleepless night and was miserable and lonely. The next morning I made up my mind that what ever comes my way I will deal with the situation. After all, this was my choice to be here.

Phu Bai Base was the pits. It had a hard surface north/south runway like Marble, and PSP used for taxiways and revetment areas. There were only a few paved roads around the base; most of them were just deep ruts in the loose dirt. When the choppers taxied in and out of the revetment area, the dust and sand could be blinding. Sand/dust storms were common on windy days, and in the heat of the summer, huge hot thermals would break from the ground and lift a cloud of dust 30 yards in diameter. When it rained, the dirt turned to mud so deep that it was almost impossible to get through.

The chow mess hall was exactly that, a mess! The typical cuisine was chicken, deep-fried to a black crisp sitting in cold oil, piled in a Bain-Marie. The vegetables were cooked to mush. Unrecognizable assorted tid-bits completed the selection. Other than the meat, everything was either canned or powdered. It was revolting, but I ate it anyway and realized that the grunts lying in rice paddies, eating rations, would love to have this food!

The City of Hue was a real hot spot for about a month during Tet Season (Chinese New Year) in February 1968. The VC took control of Hue and then killed thousands of civilians. The RVN troops were unable to take it back and General Westmoreland ordered U.S. troops to recapture the city. During the next few weeks, VC rockets and American bombs leveled complete neighborhoods. In ten days of bitter combat, the VC were slowly forced to retreat from Hue City into the Citadel (old City). Throughout the next two weeks, most of the area inside the Citadel, where about two-thirds of the population lived, was constantly fired on U.S. artillery, South Vietnamese air force and brutal house-to-house combat. Approximately 10,000 people, mostly South Vietnamese civilians, were killed during the siege, including thousands of VC troops, 400 South Vietnamese soldiers and 150 American Marines.

My first visit to Hue / Phu Bai was quiet. We didn't get hit, day or night. I wondered why any self respecting VC would waste their time to lob a couple of rockets in on us? Everyone was miserable enough living in this hole! I just wanted to establish relevant contacts, get my information, and get out of this God forsaken place.

Forty-eight hours after my arrival I had made contact with the key personal associated with the OV-10 operation and had a good idea what I was facing. It was then time to move on to Quang Tri.

I hitched a ride on another gunship to visit MAG-39 / VMO-6 at Quang Tri, 40 miles north of Hue. There was always plenty of military action in one form or another around Hue, Quang Tri and up to Dong Ha. From these air bases, choppers routinely moved supplies and men into insecure areas. But this flight for me was like a sight seeing trip. I just watched the cratered ground go by before landing at Quang Tri.

Quang Tri / VMO-6 was similar to Phu Bai, but a much smaller airfield, living area and much worse conditions. The unpleasant and miserable base was positioned in the bend of a river. On the opposite side of the river was a "friendly" village. The riverbank was lined with armed bunkers, anti personal mines and razor wire. Every morning on the village side of the riverbank, the local women could be seen washing their clothes. Tall trees and coconut palms lined the river, so the actual village couldn't be seen. It looked so peaceful, like a lost paradise except for snipers in the trees taking "pot-shots" at us on a daily basis. We were ordered not to return fire, because people in the "friendly" village might get hit! Everyone on the base was pissed off at this order. You were "unlucky" if you caught a round. Most of the time we would walk quickly in "exposed areas" and if shot at, the rounds were usually at a safe distance of ten or fifteen feet away.

As a qualified sharpshooter I understood the skill required to hit a moving target and from a tree at that distance, it would be nigh on impossible as wind age and elevation had to be precise when setting the rifle sights.

The most dangerous area for sniper activity was known as "sniper alley." It was a sandy road between the hooch area and the hangars and about 500 yards from the snipers positions across the river, near the "Friendly Village." While walking to the hangars, on couple of occasions I saw the spray of sand or dirt from the impact of a round. A crack from the snipers riffle could be heard a split second afterwards. I just walked a little more quickly and would say to myself, "They can't hit a moving target."

Before my arrival to Vietnam, AiResearch didn't have any Reps at Quang Tri Air Base to assist VMO-6 with required T76 parts (Logistics Specialist) or technical assistance (Tech Rep's). A Garrett Engine Logistics Specialist, Walt Bell, arrived in Vietnam with me and went directly to VMO-6. Walt had just been discharged from the Air Force after four years of service. He was in his early twenties, tall, very thin and reserved.

Walt had been assigned a hooch on the Air Base, so I claimed a spare bunk there. A couple of the hooch corner post supports had settled in the soft sand and the floor had a drop of about 12 inches, resulting in a 15 degree lean on the building. The low side of the hooch had taken the concussion of a 122mm rocket as well and that added to the effective lean. A few of the corrugated sheets on the concussion side were slightly buckled, but since it didn't leak when it rained, no one bothered replacing them. In fact, it seemed to add little character to it. Walt made a sign reading, "**TILTIN HILTIN**" in large bold letters and placed it over the entrance. I thought the pun was quite ingenuous and applicable for our leaning (tilt), metal-sheeted roof (tin) temporary home.

I planed to use it for the remainder of my tour, as a second home and Walt made sure that no one else jumped my claim in my absence. There were no hooch maids or local workers north of Da Nang Main, which was OK by me, because Walt kept it "spit and polished." Compared to Marble it was a basic hooch with no extra conveniences like heat, means of cooking or even making a simple cup of coffee. I put an electric blanket on my shopping list to buy the next time I went to the BX (Base Exchange) at MMAB. I had a list of things to buy and take to Quang Tri on my next trip up country. I would be able to travel much lighter if I had a few personal items waiting for me at the Tiltin Hiltin and I'd be able to stay warm on the cold nights we were experiencing.

The first night in the showers was another shock. The showers were much like MMAB, but since Quang Tri was further north the November evenings were much colder and the water was icy. However, the cold water bothered me less than the putrid, rotten egg smell and the sign at the shower entrance.

CAUTION
Do not use this water to brush your teeth.
Do not take a shower with this water if you have open wounds.

Surprisingly enough, I adjusted to the stench after about a week and the invigorating shower really felt good at the end of a long, dusty day.

One day while sun bathing on a bunker next to our hooch. I heard a loud ricochet and thud as a round went into my bunker, just under me. I jumped off the bunker and took cover. Looking up, I saw a small opening in the hooches between the top of my bunker and the trees on the other side of the river. Just enough for a sniper to get an unobstructed pot shot at me. I hadn't realized I was so exposed. I decided then and there that there would be no more sun bathing for me at Quang Tri.

I stayed at Quang Tri about 12 days on my first trip, with one overnighter at Dong Ha. I began to adjust to the life, but there wasn't much to do after evening chow. The lights weren't bright enough in the hooch to read, but we could see to play solitaire or poker. So we played cards some evenings or went to the Officers Club to drink.

After 5 days at Quang Tri I decided to make the short trip to Dong Ha to see what was the situation was like. Dong Ha was about 10 miles north of Qunag Tri and only 7 miles from the DMZ. I hitched a ride on a CH-46 Sea Knight helicopter sortie, loaded with 13 grunts suited out in full combat gear. All the round windows were removed from the CH-46 and machine guns were protruding from the front window openings.

It was much more noisy than the Huey; with the loud popping of the rotor blades, high pitch whine of the two General Electric engines and gearboxes mounted above our heads. Gaping holes remained where the windows were removed and to top it off there was no soundproofing to be seen anywhere. Once again the Crew had soundproof intercom helmets and the remainder of us resorted to sticking bullets in our ears.

From the air, I could see that Dong Ha was going to be *really* camping out. When I walked down the back loading ramp of the CH-46 with civvies on, I was greeted and surrounded by smiling grunts. They acted like I was a celebrity. I didn't know how to react to all this attention! They all wanted to touch someone that didn't have stripes on their arms or gold on their collars. It seemed that touching me was like being a little closer to "The Real World or The World"; the name Americans in Nam gave to the U.S.

The perimeter at Dong Ha Marine Air Field was a "stones throw away" in any direction. Trenches were dug in everywhere, some of them large enough to accommodate covered sandbags to become "fortified nests." The strip was basically for helicopter landing, but could just accommodate a C-130. Little or no maintenance was done there on the OV's. It was primarily used as a turnaround staging area, when sorties were underway at the DMZ. I seem to remember about 600 or so Marines there to support, hold and patrol that stretch of the DMZ.

I was pleasantly surprised that the food at the officer's mess was hot and served under cover. The officers, noncoms and enlisted men each had their own mess hall. After dark the officers mess tent was used as the "O" Club. I ate my dinner and didn't even ask about taking a shower that evening. I was staying the night and leaving early the next afternoon. I decided that when I got back to Quang Tri, I would have a refreshing cold shower.

I went to the O club about an hour or so after dark. Already everyone in the place was laughing and having a good time. I purchased my ten-cent beer and took a place at one of the wooden picnic tables.

I started chatting with the officer beside me, when out of the blue, one of the officers at another table yelled, "Anybody that can't dance is a cock sucker!" Of course, everyone around me jumped up on their seats or tables and started stomping in "quick time." In the next moment, I found myself squeezed on our tabletop dancing with them!

The next thing I knew, the lights went out for some unknown reason and in the darkness everyone was pushing and shoving to get outside. I was lucky to get out without being hurt and headed back to the safety of my little "fortified nest." I wasn't too sure about the term "Officers and Gentleman" anymore?

I was still very naive and paranoid about my safety. Everyone on the base that passed me could tell that I was a cherry. "Ole salts" could spot a FNG at one glance. They only had to take one look at the new-clothes, un-tanned skin and the lack of confidence written all over the face.

The salts enjoyed telling stories of mayhem to cherries, just to see how much they could rattle their cage.

I was warned about "Sappers" who had broken through the Dong Ha perimeter under the cover night on a couple of occasions. Sappers were the enemy, carrying satchel charges strapped to their bodies. They attempted to reach a helicopter or soft target at best or at least take out a couple grunts when they blew themselves up.

We had a couple of incoming mortars from Charlie that night and I heard some machine gun fire, but since there were no Sappers, I had a pretty good sleep all in all.

By the time I departed Dong Ha the next afternoon, I had decided to use Quang Tri as my base when up north. That's where a majority of the OV's would be for maintenance. Dong Ha was only a line of defense with a couple of OV-10s from time to time. If required, I could make it there and back in the same day if there was a major engine problem. Not only that, Dong Ha was truly "roughing it" and I knew I had a long way to go before I got back to the "Real World." Dong Ha just wasn't my cup of tea when it came to comfort and safety. I also felt that the isolation of the bases in the far north and the maintenance problems would require another Rep to support Quang Tri, Phu Bai and Dong Ha.

It seemed like I'd been away for a month rather than twelve days. I was still feeling my way around, but in some strange twisted way, I was actually enjoying the experience.

Dong Ha Base Perimeter

I was sitting on an engine container waiting for a ride to Marble at the Quang Tri helicopter landing pad

Marble Mountain Air Field From The Ground

China Beach Eastern Perimeter, looking south to The Marble Mountains.

Typical line of hooches in the NCO living area.

OV-10 Departure from MMAF

Flying Around MMAF in an OV-10

MMAF off the left hand wing tip.

Off the right wing tip, the Monkey Mountains spread east to the Sea.

Traveling Up Country

Following the coastline north; just north of Hai Van Pass.

Following the Perfume River north, just a few miles south of Hue.

Hue / Phu Bai Airport

Hue / Phu Bai Airport Terminal. Waiting to board the C-130.
I was standing on the loading ramp of the C-130 when I took this photo.

Hue Market

Entance to a Hue Market. Note the RVN guard at the entrance on the right

Basics are sold in this area. The food market is in the backround bulding.

Children in Hue

Beggar boy climbing a tree in the Hue Citidel

Beggar boys on the sidewalk, both had fallen asleep.

Hue Sights

Pregnant woman shopping in traditional dress.

Fishermen ("Charlies Navy") on the Perfume River

Hue Sights

*Just finished
praying in an empty
Christian Church*

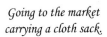

*Going to the market
carrying a cloth sack.*

Hue Citidel (Old City)

Hue, Along the Perfume River

Left:
Thien Mu Pagoda
on the banks of the
Perfume River.
Built in 1601

Right: Sampans at
rest in one of
the canals that
feed into the
Perfume River.

Hue bridge on Highway 1, heading north to Quang Tri

Huey Sorties

Above: Getting ready to taxi to the active runway.
Note the OV-10 taxiing into position for take off.

Sortie along the Perfume River, just south of Hue.

Quang Tri / VMO-6

Above: Quang Tri Air Base (VMO-6 Maintenance Facility).
Note the OV-10 parked in the hangar.
"Sniper Alley" can be seen on the right center of the photo.

Walt Bell (left) and Don Shmitt (right) at the "Tiltin Hiltin"

Quang Tri Air Base

Living Area in Windy Conditions: photo taken from "Sniper Alley"

Bunker at river perimeter overlooking the "Friendly Village"

Quang Tri Perimeter

River perimeter bunker with razor wire buffer.
Note the look out towers in the backround along the perimeter.

Notice the razor wire along the river in the foreground and the local women
washing clothes in the center of the photo.

Chapter 4
Making a Home at Marble Mountain

Before I went "up country", I bought two portable radio tape players at the BX. I sent one back to Doris and kept one for myself. It was easier to record my thoughts rather than writing. I tried to make a tape each night, as most of the other men in our hooch did. It made me feel good knowing that my three young kids would be able to hear my voice and hopefully, it would help them remember me. I wanted them to know that I missed and loved them dearly. I would be able to hear their voices too. I tried not to dwell on it, but I was really starting to miss them. Then the guilty feelings cut into me like a knife and I thought, what would it be like if I was divorced?

My oldest daughter, Donna was now the tender age of 9. She had always wanted an abundance of my attention and love and I was always ready and eager to give it. She was quite intelligent and had great insight. We had a very close relationship until the year before I left when I started seeing her draw away from me. I felt she could sense the strain between her mother and me, and she seemed to be taking it personally.

My son Douglas was just 6 and didn't seem to be aware that there were any problems between Doris and me. He always seemed to take things in his stride and was never a problem. He was born on Father's Day and that made him even more special to me. My only son, I loved him so much.

Denise, my youngest daughter, was only four. She was the most fantastic, even-tempered little girl that anyone could ask for. Never a problem from Denise! She was the smartest of the three and I believed that she had a bright future. I hardly ever knew she was around because she was so well behaved, very quiet and she smiled all the time.

Before I departed for Vietnam I had only spent about two months out of the last ten with Doris and the children in Columbus, Ohio. The other eight months, I was preparing for my assignment hundreds or thousands of miles from them. I had also come to the conclusion during this time that I was extremely unhappy within my marriage.

I contemplated divorce and how it would affect Doris and my children. It wasn't going to be easy. During the ten years of our marriage my interests had grown and Doris' hadn't. She wanted nothing more than to be a housewife and mother. Doris didn't like school and had no interest in furthering her education, or in world events. We married before she finished high school so I felt obligated to assist her in obtaining a high school diploma. I knew that if Doris didn't further her education it would be impossible for her to help support herself if I left, or the children if I was killed in Vietnam.

Doris was aware that I would be more obligated to her if she was totally dependent on me. All she wanted was to be married to me and have my children. She smothered me with love to the point of embarrassment. I needed to get away so I could see and think more clearly. I had a lot of things to work out in my mind. The money I could save in Vietnam would enable me to afford a divorce if I came to that decision. I had left Doris and the children in 1968 when I went to train for the new job in Phoenix but the guilt was overwhelming. I missed my kids too much and decided to try a little harder. I was confused and my decisions would swing wildly from day to day. One day it was the only solution and the next a divorce seemed unbearable. How could I abandon a loving wife with three young kids?

Being in Vietnam for the six months would give me time to think and Doris time to become more self-reliant. Just before I departed for Vietnam, I convinced her to enroll in an accounting course. She really didn't want to do it, but she was good at math. I thought it would divert her attention from me as well as provide her with the means to earn a living. Even so, she was very reluctant to move out of her role as a homemaker.

Since the terms of my contract provided an insurance policy with Lloyds of London for US$250,000, I felt comfortable, that in the event of my death in Vietnam, this would supplement Doris's income and the children would be financially well taken care of in the long term.

****

At Marble the civilians had about four hooches sandwiched between the NCO's and the officers' hooches. Soon after my return from up country, a bunk became available in the same civilian hooch as Jack Norton and Elroy Ackerman. It had a location identification of "161 Rocket Avenue." It was a lucky break for me to be quartered in the same hooch with two Garrett AiResearch Reps.

Jack and Elroy were assigned to Marble Mountain Air Base on a six-month contract. Both Jack and Elroy had an Air Force background and were at least ten years older than me. They arrived with the OV-10s and in a short time became "old salts." They had each purchased new 90cc Honda motorcycles to travel around the base. For a bottle of whisky or a small amount of MPC, a person could arrange just about anything.

I had to "buy in" the hooch from another departing Rep. For his investment I paid about US$60 and received all his vested interests in the hooch and some personal property. The package consisted of the bunk, clothes closet, fan, sheets, pillow and towels. All military personnel were issued their gear by the government. Civilians had to buy their gear from each other, or the base PX/BX.

My basic salary was $900 per month, three to four times more money than most Marines. As an incentive, I was paid an "Overseas Bonus" of 25%

and "Hazardous Duty/War Zone Pay" of 25%. This brought my pay to a total of $1350 per month, almost twice the amount of money I had made the year before! In addition, I was given a per diem of $12 (tax free). All civilians paid about $35 per week for three meals a day at the mess hall, which I thought was pretty cheap. The Marines at Marble had pretty good chow by military standards and we could count on a huge barbecued steak every Sunday. Of course, eating at the officers chow hall meant our food was head and shoulders above the enlisted men's.

I got along with most Marines, from the top to the bottom, even if I was called a "mercenary" from time to time. Most of the officers and noncoms called the civilians "mercenaries", as many were there for the money, rather than "the cause." The only true mercenaries were the ROK "Rock" Marines. They were from the Republic of Korea and were paid for each enemy they killed. They took no prisoners. They had a bag tied to their belt and in it were the ears of their victims that they exchanged for money.

During the first week in my new home at 161 Rocket Avenue I did two important things to improve my living conditions. My first was to purchase an electric blanket for my bunk. It was good year round. In the winter it kept me warm and in the humid summer I could turn it off a few hours before sacking out, and the mattress would be dry. I'd also have a fan running at my bedside every summer night so even when it rained for weeks at a time, I had a dry bed.

The second thing I did was to put a 100-watt bulb in the bottom of my wooden wall closet. Then I drilled about eight, two-inch holes in the back wall of the closet near the top and on the bottom. This allowed the cooler air to enter from the bottom then rise to the top when heated by the bulb and exit through the holes at the top. It kept my clothes dry and they didn't get moldy. They didn't stay dry for long but it felt good when I put them on in the morning. Dry clothes, what a luxury!

The other improvements to the hooch included a covered screened in back-porch facing the runway, about 200 yards from the threshold. Six men could sit comfortably and watch the aircraft landing in the foreground, with the beauty of the sunset in the background. This was a worthwhile evening of entertainment.

The previous occupants of the hooch had a small fridge, coffee percolator and hot plate. We could make tea or cook up some light meals or noodles. It was like moving into the Hilton after weeks of camping out in the transient hooch.

The officers chow hall was within 100 yards of our hooch and a stones throw from the eastern perimeter beach. Built onto the beach end of the chow hall, was the Officers Club. An outdoor movie "flick" would be shown on the beach side of the O club wall, two or three times a week. On dry evenings that was my entertainment.

The officer's breakfast couldn't have been better or more plentiful if we had eaten at the Hilton. The cooks did an outstanding job cooking for so many people. Every morning we could choose from cereals, yogurt, canned and fresh fruits, eggs as you like them, toast, hash browns, sausage, bacon and the old reliable "shit on the shingle." "Shit on the shingle", or SOS, was a term to describe a concoction that I've never eaten outside the military. It was made with fried ground pork, broken up into small pieces, mixed with the gravy from the drippings and poured over a couple slices of burnt toast. It tasted pretty good, but was probably as unhealthy as anything you could put in your mouth. I would usually have a big breakfast and take some fresh fruit back to the hooch for lunch.

The pissers were strategically placed around the base. They consisted of a 55 gal drum perforated with holes and buried in the sand with the top slightly above ground level. PSP provided a walkway for access in most cases. A three sided, waist high corrugated steel surrounded the buried drum, barricade for limited privacy. Standing at our pisser I could watch the aircraft takeoff and land and after dark and witness flares slowly descending at the western perimeter. You needed a strong stomach and your nose high in the air in the heat of the day. The pissers would usually fill to the brim then overflow in the wet season. Lime was spread around the outside diameter of the drum in an attempt to kill some of the odors. It didn't seem to work that well.

Our crapper was a "six-holer" with no privacy, located about 40 yards from our hooch. A single door, wooden framed, corrugated steel walled shack, with three holes close together on one side and three holes on opposite side of the small structure. A large drum positioned under each hole for easy removal of the waste by the unlucky "honey dipper". No lights were to be found in the crapper, so at night a flashlight was a necessity. It was the one place that no one spent much time. I never saw anyone reading a book in the crapper. You did your business and got the hell out of there.

I was fortunate to get into this hooch, as it was set up to accommodate five men rather than six or more. My living area was first on the left as you entered the front door, then Jack Norton's and the last area on that south wall the make shift kitchen. Opposite me was Joe Houston then Elroy Ackerman and finally Jerry Harden.

Jack and I made friends at first hand shake. Jack had retired from the Air Force after 25 years of service. Most of his career he was spent as a flight engineer on a Super Constellation, tracking typhoons while in the eye of the storm. He was very intelligent and knew the military ropes. Jack was a little rough around the edges from so many years in the military. He walked with a funny stroll, like he had bursitis in his heels. Jack could talk the leg off a steel pot. He was in his early forties and married to a refined wealthy New Englander, and they had no children. Jack and Barb were like chalk and cheese, but got along famously. Jack was a happy man. I couldn't understand why he was in Nam, but figured it was because his first love was airplanes.

Ack was very friendly and always seemed to have a smile on his face. His face was badly pitted, probably by teenage acne. He always had his hair cut to a flat top crew cut. In the evening he stood out in the crowd with his plaid sport shirt or pants and puffing on an unfiltered cigarette. Because Ack spent so much time in his bed, on his back reading a book and smoking; we dubbed him, "Mattress Back Ack."

Joe was the Lycoming engine Rep and Jerry was the Bell helicopter Rep. Jerry and Joe had something in common because the Lycoming Turbine Engines powered the Bell Huey and Cobra. I was confronted with the fact there was friction between Jerry and Joe. Joe was useless as a Lycoming Rep therefore Jerry had to do his job and didn't have much good to say about him. In fact, none of us did.

Joe, a single man, had been at Marble for two or three years and was "going tropo!" He looked like he was an officer in the Marines with his military uniform and skin haircut. He always had a cigar in his mouth except when eating and sleeping. He was afraid to fly or leave the base and knew little or nothing about the Lycoming Engines he was supporting. He stayed on the best side of the Base Commander. The men on the flight line or engine shop didn't even know that there was a Lycoming Rep on the base! Joe was very private and had his 7 x 10 foot area walled in with bare plywood, insulated, and secured with a pad lock. Inside his living area, he had a window air conditioner and a TV. Da Nang Main Air Base had a military TV station and would transmit replays of popular shows from the U.S., like "Laugh In".

Jerry was short, in his mid thirties, balding and was a little over weight. He enjoyed having a good time drinking with his buddies almost every evening at the NCO or O Club. He had the same type of partitioned room as Joe, with air conditioning and TV. Jerry had purchased this from the previous Bell Rep. Joe and Jerry were happy with their closed in rooms, because they could enjoy complete privacy and it kept the rats out of their personal items. To the envy of all of us, the Bell Reps in Vietnam had something that no other Reps had, their own Jeep! Jerry only drove it around the base, to get back and forth to the flight line.

On a cold wet night shortly after my move to Rocket Avenue I woke with a shock. I was sleeping in my warm bunk when I became aware of something scratching my right leg. I reached down in the daze of sleep, to feel my leg and find out what was wrong. I detected something warm and furry. I jumped from the bed to see a blur of fur. A rat was trying to stay warm and found a great place to snuggle up for the night!

I discovered I would have to adjust to the rats. There was no way to keep them out of the hooch. At night they would run along the windowsills just above our heads. One night we all woke up to a bloodcurdling scream, only to discover someone in a panic attack when a rat decided to take a short cut across his face to get from the floor to the windowsill.

The U.S. Government hired local men and women as laborers. They could be seen every day filling sandbags for bunkers, digging trenches and cleaning. We had a full time hooch-maid, as did most of the officers and noncommissioned men. The enlisted men were not allowed a hooch maid, as there had been problems of sexual harassment reported in the past. The maids were paid decently by local standards. The five of us paid our hooch maid about $60 a month in total. Military trucks would make pickups around Da Nang at designated stops every morning. The locals would arrive as we were leaving in the morning for the flight line and had left by the time we got back in the late afternoon. I would normally only see the maids at the hooch when we returned at lunchtime.

Local maids often ended up more of a problem than they were worth. I would rather not have had one, but the base policy was to help the locals any way you could. Missie Bai had been working for our hooch a couple of weeks before I moved in. When she started she was conscientious and a good worker. Gradually, we taught her such things as not to use the same rag to wash the coffee cups as she used to scrub the floor. New maids had a hard time adjusting and some never did. There was the problem with the quantity of soap and bleach used to wash our clothes. The Vietnamese way to wash clothes was to walk on them, in a tub of water. They didn't have soap or bleach and when given it, they didn't know how to use it. They were under the assumption that the more soap and bleach used the less they had to stomp on the clothes. Onetime, everyone in our hooch developed terrible skin rash that was unbearable in hot humid weather. The maid had used a full box of soap in one pan of washing and hung the clothes without rinsing them in fresh water!

As soon as a new maid got to know us a little more, she would ask one of us to buy soap or cigarettes for her from the BX and then sell them on the black market. The maids would also check our pockets for money. If they found any, they would take a small amount figuring it wouldn't be missed unless every cent was accounted for. It was hard to blame the girls as they were trying to get as much as they could in the short term. Many were trying to support families and would do anything for a few extra dollars. The maids referred to prostitutes on a regular basis as "cyclo girls" and say, "cyclo girls are number ten!" The maids couldn't see that they, or at least some of them were doing the same thing, surviving.

After a couple of months, Missie Bai became very lazy. She would sit around most of the day preparing her food and cooking her lunch. She also had a set ritual of caring for her very long hair. Every day she would unwind, comb and re-roll her hair into a bun. Little work would get done except the very basics. I became sick of trying to hassle the maid to do her job, but finally realized why she had become so complacent. In a loud voice with all the hooch mates present I asked, "Who's screwing the hooch maid!" No one would admit to it, but the general consensus was that someone was. It was definitely time for a replacement maid. After a new maid had been selected, the cycle would begin and end as previously, usually thanks to Joe or Jerry.

In "I" Sector, the officers on base reinforced the dangers of going outside the perimeters. I was still like a sponge absorbing the new surroundings "in country." I continued to worry about *my* bullet from Charlie, or friendly child carrying a grenade with my name on it. As a result, I stayed close, within the confines of the bases I visited.

Every night, when the mortars would come in (incoming), I would get out of bed and run to the safety of the bunker. The next day the casualties were evident. They suffered from broken legs, sprained ankles, head injuries and cuts of every description. In almost every case it was not due to shrapnel, but accidental injuries while attempting to reach the safety of their bunkers. This phenomenon was commonly known as "bunker rash."

Our hooch mates built our bunker tight against one side of our hooch, with a trap door cut in the middle of the floor, and an underground passage leading into the bunker. This way we didn't have to run outside and take a chance of getting hit with shrapnel. Inside the bunker, we each had our flack jackets, steel helmets, gas masks and spare M16's. We felt prepared, even if the base was overrun with un-friendlies.

Charlie was probably laughing his ass off because one mortar had the majority of the base scrambling for their bunkers. Most of the time mortars arrived in 30second intervals. The first mortar got everyone out of bed and running to the bunkers. The second round caught people out in the open making their way to a bunker. Since the attacks usually came after midnight it created bunker rash, lack of sleep and during the day, short tempers and mistakes.

Gradually I learned to detect, even when asleep, the difference between incoming mortars or rockets. Rockets exploded with a loud "crack" and mortars were more muffled. After a couple of months, if mortars came in during the night, I didn't even roll over. The next morning, my hooch mates, would harass me about not running to the bunker for cover. I would just look at them and smile. I could safely ignore the incoming mortars at Marble, but I couldn't be slack at any other base in "I" Sector. At Marble a routine day with no dramas, was like any military base in the U.S. except people had an "I don't give a shit happens to me" attitude.

My routine was to get out of the rack at about 6 AM, when it was relatively cool, and make a mad dash to the shower before it was full of white bodies and dirty water. Jack Norton would usually be right beside me. I would return to the hooch, get dressed and head for morning chow.

Upon my returned to the hooch, I grabbed my clipboard and left for the one mile ride on the back of Jack's Honda to the flight line. Ack was usually still in bed reading a novel.

I usually spent the first couple of hours with Jack on the flight line recording engine flight times, and daily pilot squawks, answering questions, and assisting with engine diagnostics. By the time Jack and I made our way around the flight line and arrived at the CER (complete engine repair) shop, Ack would be there, as enthusiastic as usual. He was a little eccentric in his approach, to problem solving, but he was reliable and did his best.

Ack was responsible for expediting the T76 engines through the CER shop. One of my duties was to advise Ack if an engine was coming in for repair and exactly what work it needed. Ack would rely on me when any unusual or difficult engine problems were encountered.

The CER shop at Marble was the only one in Vietnam and was capable of replacing the entire compressor and turbine-rotating group as a "rotor assembly." Therefore when an engine was repaired for low power, it was stripped without inspection and the compressor / power section parts and rotor assembly were replaced with new. We had an engine test trailer behind the shop to establish new torque pressure base lines, power output and integrity.

All the engine accident investigation was done in this shop also and I would usually be called on to head up the investigation and write the findings report.

By mid day, Jack, Ack and I would head back to the hooch. To keep in shape, I would jog up the sandy beach perimeter in my bare feet each day during lunchtime. Unless it was monsoon season, the days were usually sunny, hot and humid. The beach was deserted and I loved the solitude of my own company to let my mind drift back to the question of what I was going to do with my life!

Mornings and afternoons work schedule at Marble were much the same; I gathered information and wrote reports. In the Ops Room, the aircraft were listed on a large board on the wall. Scribbled on the board was the status of each aircraft. Beside the aircraft tail number was the name of the pilot/s flying it. My job was to find out why any aircraft was AOG and get it back to a flying status if it was an engine problem.

About 20 OV-10's were at Marble and usually five or more were grounded for one reason or the other. The lack of available parts was a big problem. We were always cannibalizing one of the grounded aircraft to get another back to a "Ready" condition. Damage from ground fire was reason for grounding an aircraft or engine removal. The "metal benders" were pretty good at doing a quick patch on the airframe to get it back in the air again.

I was starting to get an idea of the life span of the T76 engines operated by the 1st Marine Air Wing. The engines were lucky if they reached 300 to 400 hours of flight time and many didn't reach 100 hours before they were "cactus." Most of the time they were rejected or removed for low power. The cause of the low power was due to either exceeding the Exhaust Gas Temperature (EGT) limit causing excessive heat erosion of the hot section / turbine parts, or the compressors were eroded by sand ingestion.

Each mission was of the highest priority and placed above the treatment of the engines. Needless to say, the engines were abused beyond their design capability. In many cases the OV was overloaded/overweight with ordinance. There was no engine EGT limiting system and the pilots would add enough fuel, disregarding the EGT limit, to obtain the Torque/HP required to get the overweight OV off the ground. Over a period of time, the engines were pushed until the pilot was unable to make a take off, then the engine was rejected and replaced.

I hadn't realized just how abrasive the sand would be. For example, my new pair of "GI" boots lasted me no more than six weeks before the heels and soles were completely worn out. I bought a pair of soft sole "Hush Puppies" at the BX as a replacement and they lasted more than six months. The material used in the heels and soles of the Hush Puppies must have been superior to the rubber in the military boots, so most all the civilians I knew wore them. I sent samples of the sand from Marble back to the U.S. to have it analyzed and found it was one of the most abrasive silicon they had ever tested. It was no wonder the compressors eroded so quickly.

Sometimes I was required to go on test flights in a Bronco. Some engine problems or tests could not be verified during ground operation. On one occasion, during a flight test of the OV-10, I was close enough to witness OV's in action. It was awesome! I had never been in actual combat while flying in an OV-10 but I had a good idea of what it would be like. All the OV-10 support action with the maneuvers and strafing was practiced during the test flights.

Although I flew from the back seat, I always managed to get some "stick time." It seemed like every time I went out with a different pilot he would try to make me sick or black me out from pulling excessive "G loads." The OV-10 could be flown from the back seat but a landing was difficult due to the restriction of visibility from the front seat. After a number of flights I was given a certificate of accomplishment for flight-proficiency.

The OV-10 Bronco was designed to be used as a reconnaissance aircraft, to fly at low airspeeds and search for enemy ground movement. When any movement was spotted, white phosphorus rockets were fired from the pod to mark the target. F-4's would usually arrive shortly thereafter to drop napalm on the identified target.

The Broncos had "zero gravity" ejection seats installed when a pilot was required to bail out. A "D Ring" was located between your legs, just under the front of each cockpit seat. When the "D Ring" was pulled, an explosive charge was set off under the seat. The seat, with a person strapped to it, made a quick exit to clear the aircraft and tail section. Enough explosive charge is in the seats to be ejected high enough into the air for the parachute to open and carry them back to ground safely.

If the pilot elected to eject before the AO (Observer/Pilot), the back seat would fire first to clear the aircraft, otherwise the person in the back seat would get "cooked" from the blast of the exiting front seat. If the "D" ring was pulled from the back the AO seat would depart independently as there was no danger to the front seat pilot. Caution was to be used to make sure the pins were installed in the "D Ring" handles while the aircraft was not in use. If the "D Ring" was pulled accidentally with someone in the cockpit, the chances are he would be dismembered from the blast.

My Living Area at 161 Rocket Avenue Marble Mountain Air Field

In and around our hooch @161 Rocket Ave, MMAF

Entrance to 161 Rocket Ave (bunker to right)

Back entrance to 161 Rocket Ave. (Built-on shower house, left of hooch.)

Life at 161 Rocket Ave

Jack Norton
making an audio
tape to wife, Barb

Elroy Ackerman
("Mattress Back Ack")

Missie Bai
washing clothes

MMAF Hooch Maids

At 161 Rocket Ave. Missie Bai, left, with a look of envy.

One of the NCO's hooch maids

Dusk and Sunset from 161 Rocket Ave MMAF

Day to Night around MMAF

Evening entertainment in the "O" Club.
Top right photo: Bar Girl serving
Officers during the entertainment.

Complete Engine Repair "CER" Shop and Test Trailer

T76 in Transport and
engine build stands

T76 Engine installed
in the test trailer and the
engine maintenance crew.
(Richard Ingelido far right)

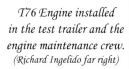

Mechanics working
on a T76 in an engine
build stand.

OV-10 in the news at MMAF

MMAF Flight Line

Pilot "preflight". Note the North American Rep in the foreground.

Unattended rockets and ammo on the tarmac.

Prepairing the OV Flight Crew and Aircraft Ready for Flight

Above: Preparing pilots
for an OV-10 Mission

Left: Maintenance Chief does
a final check before signing
the OV off as "flight ready".

Retrieved OV-10

Notice that twisting of the propeller indicates that the engine was running at a high power when the aircraft made contact with the ground.

Ack inspecting the crashed OV-10

Some of the Different Aircraft Operating from MMAF

Lockheed C-130 "Hercules"

Fairchild C-123

Bell "Cobra" Gunship

Boeing Vertol CH-47 "Shithook"

Pilatus Porter U.S. Registered (CIA?)

Boeing CH-46 "Sea Knight"

Sikorsky CH-53 Cargo

Bell "Huey" Gunship

F-4 "Fantoms" at Da Nang Main Airport

On The Way To Da Nang City

Farmer's hut with hay stack along side.

Local Danang bus stop, heading north on Highway 1.

Downtown Da Nang City

One of the main streets in Da Nang. Note the RVN Jeep on patrol.

Local markets in Downtown Da Nang. Note the RVN with the bike on patrol.

Photos Taken From Monkey Mountain

Looking North from Monkey Mountain

Looking South from Monkey Mountain. A fantastic view of China Beach stretching to the Marble Mountains in the background.

China Beach Orphanage

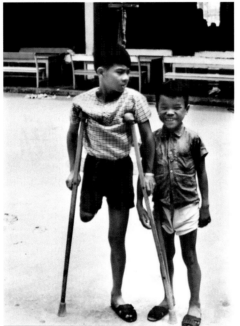

Chapter 5
Changing Attitudes

Not long after my arrival in Nam, Jack introduced me to the Supply Sergeant who had connections at Kadina Air Base in Okinawa. The most important thing about the Military is "Connections." You scratch my back and I'll scratch yours. Bartering was the name of the game. I gave the Sergeant a bottle of whiskey and enough MPC to buy a new 90cc Honda for me. About three weeks later the Honda arrived at Marble. I was so happy that I gave the Sergeant another bottle! I felt like chains had been removed and was thrilled to have complete mobility. It was a special feeling for me, riding the new Honda down the road for the first time. I was enjoying the warm wind blowing on my face and through my hair. It was the freedom not many others could appreciate. At that time no helmet or license was required on the base. Later, the Base CO passed the word that, while on base, helmets would be worn, but there was still no requirement for a license plate or registration on or off base.

One of the best things about Marble was China Beach. The beach was clean and what I considered to be safe. I enjoyed the solitude and it allowed a brief escape from the war. Getting to the beach however, was like going though a maze. First, you had to go through the chain link fence at the perimeter, then zig zag through the land mines and barbed or razor wire that stretched the distance of the beach perimeter parallel to the fence line. Once on the beach, looking north or south as far as the eye could see, there was open space and white sand. The only structure on the beach was a white observation tower with a Grunt Life Saver in swimming trunks and an M16 by his side! From the beach looking back over the chain link fence, spaced every few hundred yards, were manned and heavily armed observation towers overlooking the South China Sea.

Vietnamese fishermen could always be seen bobbing around on the water. They stayed more than a couple hundred yards from the beach line; otherwise a few rounds would be fired over their heads if they were lucky! Woven boats, shaped like a disk about 8 to 10 feet in diameter were used and somehow, they could stand and throw a huge circular fishing net into the sea, then pull in their catch. We called them Charlie's' Navy!

One week, windstorms and heavy rain kept me from my normal trips to the beach. When the storm subsided I was anxious to take advantage of the first clear, day, however I found the beach entrance gate secured with a guard. From where I was standing at the barbed wire, I could see a couple of Marines walking on the beach swinging something back and forth over the sand. A couple others were crawling along next to them. The guard told me that they were using metal detectors to look for anti-personal land mines. He further explained that early that morning someone noticed a land mine uncovered by the storm. The bomb squad subsequently detected or uncovered five more mines. It gave me a warm all over feeling, like I pissed myself! No one knew how long the mines had been there, but one thing for sure, the Marines didn't plant them. Charlie's Navy had apparently slipped onto the beach one dark rainy night and buried them. I had been running up and down the beach with no idea of the dangers under foot.

Everyone on the base was warned not to enter the water at this time of the year. Sea snakes were breeding, very aggressive, and very poisonous. I didn't know of anyone who had been bitten by a snake but had seen a few swimming on the top of the water just off the beach while I was jogging.

A couple of days after the beach was cleared of land mines, I was jogging in my usual state of mindlessness. There was some excitement about 50 yards down the beach and I noticed a man about 20 yards off shore yelling, "snake!" and calling for help. People on the beach were reluctant to attempt a rescue, knowing the snake was close by. Finally a couple of brave souls ran into the water, grabbed the man and brought him back to the beach. The Marine Captain was already dead after a single bite to the neck. There was nothing any of us could do about it. A couple of the lifeguards went off to get a stretcher and I decided that I had enough jogging for the day and went back to my hooch.

So many different tragic events were happening each day; that I felt myself losing compassion and becoming numb to the fact that there was danger everywhere. I saw young men go out in their flying machines; never to return, but to die by snake-bite is not what one expects in a war.

Towards the end of the week of rain, we had more "incoming" than ever before. I later learned that during the heavy rains the VC used water buffalo to move the 122mm, 140mm rockets or 81mm mortars into strategic positions and concealed them for later use. Our observation aircraft were limited in patrolling the outer perimeter in the heavy rains and the VC could position the rockets undetected.

On clear nights and OV-10 Bronco or O-1 Bird Dog observation aircraft would watch for "ground flashes". This would reveal the location of the mortars or rockets fired by the VC. The aerial observation would contact Puff by radio, then lasers from an OV would mark the "flash position", and Puff would lay the spray of molten lead over the area.

Grunts went out one morning after Puff had made some passes the night before and found the body of a local base barber. Without detection, the VC barber apparently had been on the base to identify potential targets and assist the VC in dropping shit in on us. It was another reminder that it was probably no more dangerous to be off base than on. I was getting past the paranoia of what I describe as Stage One and developing the, "I don't give a shit attitude", of "Stage Two." In Stage One, I had worried about seeing Christmas. Now, I was almost certain I wouldn't live to see the end of my tour. I had a warped sense of time and reality. Que Sera Sera!

I lived from one day to the next, without thinking much about it. Every day on the flight line something unpredictable happened. Sometimes we were lucky, sometimes we weren't.

One maneuvering technique to mark or attack a target was a high-speed dive from a safe altitude. In the dive the pilot could line up, lock on the target, fire the ordinance and pull out, before hitting the ground. Sometimes a pilot would be so fixed on the target that he would forget his altitude and pull out too late; driving straight into the ground. "Target affixation" as it was known, was a common occurrence.

One day a pilot called the tower to clear the runway for an emergency landing. After a safe landing, I went out to the revetment to debrief the pilot. I couldn't believe the damage to the aircraft. Deep indentations were in the leading edges of the wings and tail. A piece of limb from a tree was wedged in the tail. The tops of the wings were buckled from exceeding the "G Limits." The props on both engines were severely bent. Both engines had bent first stage compressor impellers and I could smell burnt wood coming from the engine inlet and tail pipe. There was no doubt in my mind that the pilot had flown into the tree tops, and was very lucky to fly out of them, as there was no evidence of being hit with ground fire. The pilot admitted to me that he had suffered from target affixation and had exceeded the G limits of the aircraft to pull out at the bottom of the dive! Somehow he managed to bounce through the treetops and maintain enough airspeed to climb out to a safe altitude to return back to Marble. The two pilots couldn't say enough good things about the OV-10 from that day on. Any other aircraft or engines would not have been as forgiving.

When the two engines were removed, and disassembled at the CER shop we found them packed with burnt sawdust. How they ran after so much ingestion, I'll never know. I have seen engines in much better condition than these and not run at all. The props were bent so badly; I couldn't understand how the engines stayed together from the vibratory loads, or that the vibration didn't tear the engines from their wing mounts. I believe the Wings of Angels brought them back safely.

Another OV-10 arrived and I was asked by one of the excited ground crew to, "take a look at this!" I climbed into the cockpit and closed the canopy. The Plexiglas canopy had two clean holes in it. One from the entrance of the bullet and one on the opposite side where the bullet made its' exit. It appeared the round had just missed the pilot's head. We placed a string from one bullet hole through the next, pulled it tight and taped it on the outside to see the exact path of the trajectory. Once more I crawled into the front seat and closed the canopy. With the canopy secured, I sat with my head against the headrest and the string was about one inch from the bridge of my nose. But, the pilot had a helmet on; so with that additional thickness, it meant that the round had to have come within a whisker of taking his nose or cheek. Had he been leaning forward in the seat when the round passed through the canopy, it would have taken a lot more than his nose or cheek!

Another pilot managed to land the OV in spite of having a kneecap blown off by a single round of ground fire. It entered the underside of his knee and deposited kneecap fragments all over the inside of the canopy. He lost a lot of blood but he lived to tell the tale and didn't have to fly in combat any more.

****

Unbeknown to us, there was a huge ground swell of opposition to the Vietnam War throughout the U.S. The only news for our consumption was controlled by the military to some degree. The Stars and Stripes military newspaper was distributed on a regular basis, but all was not revealed in the articles. Then there was the news on the "Good Morning Vietnam" radio station we listened to each day before going to the flight line. But again, it was censored, biased and incomplete! The evening news on the television was seen by the fortunate few in Vietnam. Again it was censored and biased.

The only true and unadulterated news came from our letters back home. In turn Joe Public in the U.S., wasn't told about the heavy drug use, drinking, racial tension, chaos, lack of morale, losses and fuck-ups going on all around us in Nam.

Fights occurred each night in the enlisted men's hooch area. No one went outside their hooch without a couple of buddies. The blacks attacked the whites and the whites would attack the blacks. The base hospital had numerous admissions from fighting, stabbing and shootings, that weren't inflicted by the enemy.

****

"Bosses Night" was held on a regular basis on Friday or Saturday night. The enlisted men invited their "boss" to come to their club in the enlisted men's hooch area. The NCO's and officers called it "The Animal Club" and I soon found out why. I wasn't their "boss" but was invited. I wasn't keen on going at night but was assured there would be "No problem."

The EM Club was located on the beach perimeter. The large stone building, covered with a corrugated sheet metal roof, was positioned on an unpainted concrete slab. Row after row of wooden picnic tables and chairs were almost hidden by the sea of Marines. It looked like pure chaos. At every table, those seated had numerous full cans of beer in front of them. A game of "liars dice" was usually played to decide who would buy the table the next round of drinks. When a round was delivered to the table, the tab on each can was snapped open by the bartender. Beer was not to be removed from the premises or taken back to the hooches. There was also a contest whereby empty cans were carefully stacked one upon another to build a pyramid in the middle of the table. The table that drank the most beer had the best chance of winning!

Large crowds around the tables indicated that chugalug contests were going on. Most of the men huddled in the tight packs were placing bets on the suspected winner. The tops of two beer cans were removed, filled to the very top with beer, and placed directly in front of the two contestants. Once all bets were placed, the referee slapped the table and said go. No beer could be spilt as the men chugalugged. I was amazed at how quickly someone could actually pour a can of beer down his throat, without swallowing. The winner took a percentage of the bets and then went outside for a couple of minutes to stick his fingers down his throat. Once his stomach was cleared, he would reappear to compete with someone else. This was serious business and a lot of MPC would change hands!

Before the night was over an argument broke out at one of the chugalug tables. The next thing I knew, one of the arguing men had knocked over a pyramid of cans at a nearby table. It seemed automatic that thing to do was to start throwing fists and everyone in the bar was fighting and throwing cans of beer. I made a quick dash for the exit, jumped on the Honda and headed back toward safe territory.

I was riding the Honda down the dark road, toward my hooch, thinking about what I had just witnessed and how the war was affecting these young enlisted men. It was a moonless night. The only light came from the enlisted men's huts as I passed by them. I was moving along at no more than 15 mph and the cool damp night air from the South China Sea felt good blowing on my face. On occasion my nostrils could detect the smell of marijuana in the air. Then it came; a whining percussion with an impacting blast of air in my left ear followed by the crack of a gunshot. I have no words to explain my feelings at that moment, or the sound as the bullet passed within millimeters of my ear. I quickly pulled off the road and ditched the Honda, on its side in the soft sand and I ducked behind it for cover.

Someone had taken a shot at me and was trying very hard to do me the maximum amount of damage. I wondered if the base had been over run while I was in the animal club, or if it was one of our own? I didn't have my 45 and just lay there looking for some movement in the darkness. It never occurred to me that I would need to carry a weapon in the safe confines of the base.

I was feeling extremely confused, exposed and uncomfortable. I saw a speeding Jeep with MPs, came to an abrupt stop a couple of huts from where I was lying. A spot light from the Jeep was fixed on a position between the huts and I saw an MP disappear among the mass of corrugated hooches. Another MP ran to see if I was hit. While I was lifting my Honda back to an upright position, the MP told me that they had seen a muzzle blast from an M-16 and then a glimpse of a black Marine running from the scene.

The MP helped me push the Honda back onto the road and told me politely to get out of there. He reminded me of the racial tension among the black and white enlisted men and said that it was wise to travel in small groups at night, even to go to the showers or pissers. I decided not to tempt fate and stayed away from the enlisted men's' area at night from then on. There was enough danger around without inviting more!

Two OV's at Marble Mountain Air Field Taking off to the South

Chapter 6
Da Nang, Rocket City

    The following weekend I decided to check out Da Nang City. Da Nang had a reputation for taking so much heavy and routine rocket fire that it took on the nickname "Rocket City." I wasn't overly worried about getting off the base for the first time alone. It was great to truly spread my wings and not worry about what was around the corner. I dressed in a T-shirt, my shoulder holstered 45 and a loose fitting short sleeved, shirt. I gave the Honda a thorough "pre-flight" to reduce my chances of a break down. This Sunday ride to the city marked the beginning of a new phase for me. The extreme caution I had taken since my arrival in Nam was beginning to evolve into reckless behavior for the next stage of my tour. One of my pilot friends couldn't believe I would go to town by myself. He kept telling me how dangerous it was. Yet as a pilot he saw action and confronted the enemy in the air almost every day, without fear and this was his second tour in Nam!

    Very few cars were on the road as most of the locals rode bicycles or 90cc Hondas. The RVN (Republic of Vietnam) soldiers owned most of the Hondas. When I left the base I tried to blend in with the locals even though my body frame was much larger.

    The City of Da Nang and surrounding areas were off limits to all Military Personnel other than the RVN and ROK (Republic of Korea) soldiers. In the early 60's Da Nang was open to any U.S. GI with a pass. I was told the streets were alive with all night bars, GI's and prostitutes. Later Da Nang became too dangerous and was declared "Off Limits" to all U.S. military and a curfew was initiated from dusk till dawn. RVN were in control of the security of City of Da Nang and enforced the curfew. At revetment posts in and out of the City, barbed wire barricades were stretched across the roads during curfew. Barricades were also strategically placed across the City streets, without warning. I was aware that the RVN were unscrupulous and there were stories of RVN, on and off duty, shooting civilians, taking their money and blaming the VC. I didn't want to put myself into that position.

    I discovered that the central business district of Da Nang was in shambles. Most of the buildings were two-story and constructed of mortar and or hand made bricks. The paint or lime covering the rough building surface had almost disappeared. The streets were unpaved, pot holed littered with garbage. Public facilities and systems were absent or discontinued. There was no regular garbage pickup so garbage was stacked in six to eight foot piles at various street corners. The smell of Da Nang could be detected, long before arrival.

    I rode around the main streets of the downtown area and found the place full of rubble with few people to be seen. Three naked boys about three years old were standing on a street corner. As I approached them I could see smoke from the cigarettes they were puffing. I could detect western bone structure in their Vietnamese faces. I went by them slowly, gave them a big smile and waved as a friendly gesture. They looked me straight in the eye as I passed by, "flipped me a bird" and in unison yelled, "Fuck ya Geee-eye!" I was shocked and wondered if the attitude was that of their family. If they had no family that might explain their bitterness, but I struggled with the fact that these are the people the U.S. came to help, to set free so they could make their own choices! Now, it seemed they wanted to choose to be free of the Americans? I thought to myself, maybe we've been here too long already? The Americans were now seen as the aggressors. Is this what things have come to? I was very naive, but I was learning fast.

I continued to ride around the streets looking for a smiling face. I saw a woman squatting with one leg of her black pajamas pulled up, pissing in the gutter. She didn't look up from under the cone shaped hat till I was beside her, then I could see the face of an old lady smiling, mouth stained and full of betel nut. At least I got a smile from someone! I had picked the wrong day, as everything appeared to be closed. Only rats, the size of cats, were in abundance, lumbering around the stacks of maggot-infested garbage at numerous street corners. The rats seemed to be free to do anything they liked, unlike most people in this country.

I wasn't into drinking in middle of the day, but since bars had been the main attraction in the past for the GI's, I thought I'd check them out. They also seemed to be the only places open. I selected one out of the many that lined both sides of the street. As I entered, I saw a couple of girls sitting together in the booths and a male bartender behind the bar. Nothing great about the appearance of this place! The floor had broken tiles, and the concrete walls and ceiling were badly in need of a new coat of whitewash. Scattered throughout the room, in disarray, were heavily scratched tables, bare wooden chairs and wooden booths fixed to the side of one wall. A couple of ceiling fans were rotating, slow and erratic.

As soon as the girls spotted me, they were in hot pursuit. They each grabbed an arm and led me to the bar. "Buy me tea?" one said. "Maybe whiskey?" said the other smiling with a mouth full of shiny gold teeth. I ordered them each a glass of tea and asked for a beer. Much to my surprise, a can of slightly chilled Budweiser arrived for me. I was expecting a warm Ba-Moi-Ba (Vietnamese Beer). The girls were served tea in dirty whiskey shot glasses. I was a little surprised of the cost of the beer and tea when the bartender asked payment for the round of drinks. He gave me a big smile, exposing his shiny gold teeth, as the he took the money. The tea's were MPC$1.50 each which included payment for the girls company. Soon after the girls received their tea, the bartender returned and gave them each .50 cents, obviously their commission. Whiskey was priced at MPC$3 or more and the common practice was to water the girls' drinks down. Back at the Officers Club, a beer was ten cents and an unadulterated whiskey was 25 cents, therefore Da Nang bar prices were outrageous! But why complain, I thought, I have to pay for the company and the experience.

It didn't take one of the girls long to ask, "You want me? Only $5! I show you good time?" The other was quick to add, "Maybe you want special massage?" "No thank you", was my quick reply. I wasn't interested in any form of sex or the risk of contracting a dose of "cock rot". If anyone pretended to be interested, the girls would badger them and get quite upset if rejected. I respected that they were there to make a living and not to be hassled or joked about. Life was not easy for them. But on the other hand, I knew you couldn't believe anything they said, particularly when it came to money.

I had a chat with the girls and bought them a couple more teas. We had a few laughs and I finished my now warm beer, paid up and headed back to Marble. I decided the next time I went to Da Nang; I would visit the Saturday morning markets. The girls had told me that the markets were a good place to have a look around and take some pictures.

On my return to base, the girls outside the "cabbage patch" were waving for me to pull over. I kept going, but waved back. I'd had enough female company for the day. When I arrived back at the hooch, everyone was eager to know if I got laid. When I told them that I hadn't, they wouldn't believe me!

Soon after, Jack and Ack started to travel to Da Nang with me. It soon became a ritual of ours to head off to town, or just get off the base anywhere for a ride on the Hondas. We discovered an access road to Monkey Mountain, a peninsula, four to five miles off the mainland almost due east of Da Nang. The road was paved, narrow and winding through thick jungle with no inhabitants. The largest mountain was at the tip of the peninsula. We could only ride about three quarters of the way up before the 90cc Hondas bogged down from the steep incline of the mountain road.

After we returned and told our fellow Marines about the trip, they were horrified. Apparently Monkey Mountain was riddled with "dug-in" Charlie. But then whenever we asked the Marines what was safe and what wasn't, they would always reply, "Don't leave the base, you crazy bastards." However, that was the last time we made a motorcycle trip to Monkey Mountain. Maybe Charlie had that weekend off and went into town for a couple of cold beers!

Chapter 7
The Cabbage Patch

A couple hundred yards north of the Marble Mountain Air Field main gate, on the western side of Highway One, was a group of thatched huts, known as the Cabbage Patch. The huts had dirt floors, no windows and door openings covered with strings of beads or strips of plastic instead of doors. This was the local brothel or "den of iniquities" and as many as 10 to 20 girls stood at the roadside waving at every passing military vehicle. With the cities and towns off limits, many of the girls moved to the Cabbage Patch in order to survive.

In the Cabbage Patch, most of the girls had a good handle on the English language but with a heavy "jive" accent, just like the clientele they conversed with. And to top it off, the words "mother fucker" would be in just about every sentence they used.

The girls knew that the grunts would get a pass to go from Marble to a large Post Exchange (PX), just south of Da Nang City. Three quarter ton cargo trucks "four-bys" were provided for transportation to and from the PX. After shopping at the PX, they would hitch a ride back to base with a returning four-by. But a trip to the PX wasn't what many had on their mind. On a regular basis a four-by would slow to a crawl outside the Cabbage Patch and a group of grunts would jump from the back and run into the huts with girls following. They never seemed to argue about who got who. I guess that they felt there was safety in numbers; each man taking turns with the girls, then standing guard duty.

When business was completed at the Cabbage Patch, a south bound, four-by would slow and the group would jump on board to return to base. On numerous occasions, I would stop along the road at the Cabbage Patch and chat-up the girls. It was nice just to hear a female voice, even if every other word from her mouth was a four letter one.

I had been pre-warned about the severity of wild strains of VD in Vietnam before leaving the U.S. It scared me enough that, even with a few beers under my belt, I was not going to take my pants off for any kind of sex. Of course, the girls only wanted one thing in the end, money. The way to get it was to get the man into one of the huts. They had a tough and uncertain life and were just trying to survive in the most extreme circumstances. How could anyone criticize the life these girls were leading, with war on their doorstep and survival utmost on their mind.

I opted for intercourse by conversation, in itself. I noticed that if you initially started talking with one girl, the remainder of them would back off after a couple of minutes. The next time I stopped, it would be difficult to get any of the other girls to talk with me. There seemed to be a policy that a girl was able to "stake a claim to you", even if you have never had sex with them.

One cold night, I was returning to Marble from Da Nang Main Air Base on my Honda. It was past curfew, after dark and I had a few beers in me. No other vehicles were to be seen on the unlit road. As I was passing the Cabbage Patch the girls tried waving me down in a desperate attempt to get one last customer. I decided to stop for a couple of minutes. Much to my surprise, an unfamiliar girl ran over to my side. Even in the dark, I was aware of extremely large bumps under her heavy sweater! I had never seen any local girls with her chest size and guessed that she had an oversized padded bra on. The effects of the alcohol had loosened my tongue enough for me to ask if they were real or not. She insisted they were and tried to coax me to go with her by offering a lower price.

I'd had enough and was about to move on when her final offer, was to "bet" me that her breasts were real. If I lost I had to pay her the $5. I thought it would be a safe bet and was quick to agree to the wager. The next thing I knew, she had pulled her sweater over her head, revealing two huge breasts standing out without the assistance of a bra. At the blink of an eye she had me by the arm trying to pull me from the Honda and take me with her. She insisted that I lost the bet and had to go with her! I didn't think that was part of the bet! The other girls also pulled at my arms and saying, "You lost, so you **must** go with her!" The more I resisted the more and more girls gathered around me and persisted.

I decided to go, but there was no way I was going to have sex with her. I planned to go inside for a short period and pay the $5 and get the hell out of there. I was concerned about leaving my Honda outside, so I pulled it up tight to the hut entrance. I was now starting to sober up and anxious to get this over and done with.

I walked into the grass hut, dimly lit and noticed a maze of small rooms. The girl who won the bet entered the room on the left through the hanging strings of colored plastic. I followed closely behind. As my eyes were adjusting to the single candle light in the room, I could only see a couple of personal items scattered around and a tatami mat, used for a bed, on the dirt floor.

This girl wasn't accustomed to wasting time. She put her hand out and said: "$5!" I promptly paid. She proceeded to undress herself and called me to the tatami to lie down with her. I didn't take my clothes off but lay next to her. She was attempting to undress me and acted upset when I resisted. She was easy to look at and even more attractive lying there in the nude in the flickering dim light. I hadn't seen a nude woman in longer than I wanted to think about. She was probably in her early twenties, with slim features and tight dark skin. Her breasts were exaggerated from the warm reflecting candlelight. My eyes were fixed on them and I became more uncomfortable as I realized that this was not going to be as easy as I had thought. I was just about to ask her a couple of questions to take up some more time and try to figure out how to get out of this situation without creating a scene. At that moment, a young boy about 9 came charging into the room through the plastic stringers. He started yelling in excitement, "Your girlfriend is coming to kill you!"

"What do you mean, my girlfriend?" I asked, while jumping from the tamami to my feet. In the next second, a girl came crashing into the room, with a shining, long-bladed, knife in her hand. She was yelling at me, "You mother fuckar; caca dau, caca dau. I'm gonna stick you with this knife and cut your heart out, you mother fuckin butterfly!" "Caca dau, you cock suckar, you said you would fuck me, but now, you boom boom my girlfriend!" Despite the anger on her face in the dim light, I recognized her. She was the same friendly girl I normally chatted with beside the road. I realized she had staked her claim on me at our first meeting on the road. In Vietnam, if anyone cheated on their partner, they were known as a "butterfly." I was amazed that she could accuse me of being a butterfly when I had no commitment to her and she was screwing, probably, hundreds of men each week!

At first, I was in shock; but then started to verbally retaliate. She kept the knife raised and moving, as though she would strike at any moment. I didn't think I would have too much trouble disarming her, so I decided to talk first. I told her, "If you cut me, I am going to take the knife away from you and throw a grenade in the hut on my way out!" That got her attention. She lowered the knife, but continued murmuring, "You mother fucker, if you ever stop here again, I will kill you on the roadside!"

I quickly left the room as her threats continued, but I was worried that she would change her mind and come at me with the knife, still waving in her lowered hand. I started the Honda and departed in a cloud of sand and dust.

From then on, every time I passed by the Cabbage Patch, I could always spot my *girlfriend,* flipping me a bird as soon as I came into view. Even after passing her, I could see her in my rearview mirror standing on the roadside with her arm and finger high in the air. I never stopped for verbal intercourse at the Cabbage Patch for the remainder of my tour.

Chapter 8
Tis The Season to be Jolly

By Christmas, I felt like I was just going through the motions. I'd made a couple more trips up north and found that I could hardly recognize what normality was. The rainy season was well underway. Everyone was getting irritable, mostly because of the torrential rain and lack of sleep from the relentless incoming. By now, we had more than enough rain and yet expected at least another month of it.

Somehow Ack found out that there was a Children's' Orphanage on the way to Da Nang, on the beach side. When I heard of the 100 or so children with no parents and no future, I felt like I had to give the orphans something for Christmas, even if only in a small way. Jack, Ack and I decided to pitch in and buy thongs for the kids. We found out that almost all of them were running around barefoot.

Most Vietnamese always seemed to be walking in a pair of "Ho Chi Min Road Runners" as we called them. They were nothing more than a worn out military truck tire, cut to the shape of ones foot. Three holes were drilled in the cutout sole and threaded with rope or thin webbing. The rubber tread of the shoe would never wear out.

We stopped in advance at the orphanage to arrange the Christmas visit. Christmas didn't mean anything to most Vietnamese, as most were practicing Buddhists. But this Orphanage was a little different; it had been set up by a French Catholic Church and was now run by Vietnamese Nuns. The place was rundown and suffered from lack of funds. God only knows where they got the money to feed those children.

On a trip to town we bought up almost every pair of thongs and sandals at the weekend market. I didn't know if I was doing this to make myself feel better or truly help the kids. I felt sad, apprehensive and guilty before we arrived at the orphanage. As we were handing out the sandals, I could only think about how much these kids needed. It broke my heart.

They ranged in ages from a couple of months to around ten years old. They were everywhere and I felt overwhelmed. Many children were just sitting in the dirt and hallways with a blank look of despair on their faces. As I glanced around at the orphans, I felt partly responsible for their lost parents. In addition, most had suffered from gunshot or land mine wounds. Some managed to smile when the sandals were passed out or when I took their picture, but the look of hopelessness was everywhere.

A couple young boys wanted their pictures taken with their new sandals on. The shortest of the two gave me a big smile, while the other one on crutches with one leg missing above the knee, quickly turned his head away as the shutter snapped. I asked myself, "What chance do these kids have and what the fuck is really going on in this country?"

****

Since I was a civilian, per my contract, I was entitled to have weekends off. However with this type of assignment it was impossible and one day was pretty much like the rest. The only day I could identify was Sunday. On Sunday we were given a large green tablet with our chow at evening mess, to prevent a local strain of malaria. This ritual was memorable to me, because Monday morning the line at the crapper was longer than usual. After a while I decided to stop taking them. Various strains of malaria existed in Vietnam and the tablet given for the Da Nang area didn't give me any defense against the other strains. Over a period of time, one of the side effects of the preventive medication was blindness. I decided I'd rather take my chances with the mosquitoes.

I worked seven days a week. The war didn't recognize hours, days, or years for that matter. I made an arrangement with the Base Commander to accumulate weekend days to use as leave when requested. So, with more than two months in country, I was entitled to sixteen days leave so I planned to take at least ten of them.

I spent the last couple of working days leading up to Christmas at MMAB to prepare for my leave. I needed a break from the travel up country and time to catch my breath before my R&R. Things seemed to be falling into place and the military action seemed to gear down over the holidays. On the 20th of Dec I was going to fly to Cubi Point in the Philippines on the way to Hong Kong. Cubi Point/Olongapo was a U.S. Naval Base and one of the stopping off points for the Marines going to and from Vietnam. Taking a military flight to the Philippines was a cheaper way for me to get to Hong Kong. All military personal were provided with flights to their requested R&R locations at no charge. But being a civilian, I was required to pay for my R&R flights. Since the flight to Cubi Point was a military flight and not an R&R flight, I would only pay for a flight from Manila to Hong Kong and return to Manila. I had to make my own way from Cubi Point to Manila.

I was impressed with the quality of the base food leading up to Christmas, but I was going to miss the big Christmas dinner that everyone was talking about. The food would be like home: turkey, with all the trimmings, ham, mashed potatoes, gravy, cranberry sauce and for dessert, ice cream and pumpkin pie, and extra treats as well.

To top it off, the pre-Christmas celebrations included entertainment at the Officers Club almost every evening. The show consisted of about six girls in short colorful costumes, kicking their stuff and dancing to a small four-piece band. They sang some of the popular songs and there were smiles on the faces of everyone while reminiscing about "The Real World." Anytime we had live entertainment we would request two songs; "We got to get out of this place, if it's the last thing we ever do" by The Animals was the first. Everyone would join in on the chorus.

Then we insisted on, "I Want To Go Home, I Want to Go Home, Ohhh How I Wanna Go Home." When the chorus of that song was reached, all the Marines would sing at the top of their voices, "**I wanna get LAID, I wanna get LAID, OHH how I wanna get LAID!**" By the end of the song everyone would be standing on their chairs and waving their arms in the air while singing. I think the poor girls were blown away at the thought that these might be the Marine Corps finest.

Chapter 9
First Hong Kong R & R

After the Friday night show, I returned to my hooch to get packed for my departure the following morning. I lifted my suitcase down from on top of my clothes locker for the first time in almost two months. I had stored a few of my best civilian clothes, leather belt and a pair of good leather shoes in it. When I opened the case I couldn't believe my eyes. The clothes and shoes were covered with a thick mold. The case was filled to the brim with coils of green growth. I had never seen anything like it before. I quietly closed the case again, walked it outside to the garbage tip and gave it the heave ho! I would have to buy new civvies in Hong Kong.

A warrant officer, by the name of Stubbs, offered to give me a ride in a Huey slick, from MMAB to Da Nang Main, early the next morning. Stubbs was qualified for the Huey and the OV-10. I got to know him as a quiet man with a good mental attitude. This was his second tour in Nam. He had seen a lot of action and never talked much about it. When we touched down at Da Nang Main the next morning, Stubbs put the slick down about 50 yards from the C-130 I was about to board. As soon as I jumped out on a dead run from the slick, Stubbs pulled collective. He was off like he just made a troop drop-off in a hostile LZ. I was almost blown off my feet from the rotor wash not to mention the stinging gravel and sand rash. He was probably grinning from ear to ear.

I was on the manifest and had no trouble getting on board the C-130. As I looked around, I noticed I was the only civilian out of 80 or more. Everyone else was a hardcore grunt. They looked like they were on their way home and carried everything issued on their backs.

When I walked up the ramp of the C-130, I could see that this was not going to be a comfortable trip. There were no seats in the cargo aircraft; only cargo tie down straps lying on the deck. The straps were strung across from the left to the right hand side of the fuselage. We walked in and stood shoulder to shoulder with a tie down strap at our feet. We were then told to sit down on the metal deck and place our legs under the strap in front of us in a yoga position. I have no idea how many rows of straps that were laid down from the front to the rear of the cabin, but I could feel the claustrophobic sensation of being confined in a tightly formed crowd.

The C-130 cruise speed of 325 mph would normally make the 700-mile leg in about 3 hours. The metal deck was hurting my ass already, even before we got in the air. I just hoped my bladder would hold out because there were no relief tubes.

Shortly after take off, the cabin became very cold. I didn't have a damn thing to put on to keep warm. The grunts started digging out their ponchos. I should have known better since I'd flown in C-130s before and knew there was no effective heating system. Short, low level flights, below 10,000 feet weren't too bad; but a long-leg, high-elevation flight was going to be a new experience. Since this was a pressurized aircraft, it would climb and fly to the Philippines well above 18,000 feet. That meant I might freeze before I got there. I was grateful for the body heat and material from the ponchos of the grunts around me. It was a very bumpy ride for the first hour after we had leveled off. I could only guess that we were *just* above a nasty monsoon. The turbulence made for a rough flight. The tie down strap was cutting into my upper thighs and the bare metal I was sitting on tore into the cheeks of my ass. The pilots had to throttle back the C-130 to reduce air speed due to the heavy turbulence, making the trip much longer than normal.

There was not much light in the aircraft and no windows to let us see what weather we had below or around us. The bare metal of the fuselage was exposed with no soundproofing insulation and the four Allison turboprop engine aircraft sounded like a beating drum. I had my trusty 45 bullets stuck in my ears and was trying not to think about how cold I was, when all hell broke loose. Instant fog! Nothing could be seen in the dense cloud within the aircraft. Even without visibility, the fog gave off brightness like driving a car with high beams in fog at night.

Next the aircraft went into a steep dive. I could hear men yelling and loosing their composure. In the zero visibility, a couple of men ran and climbed over the others in panic. We were still diving into the bowels of the storm and the men were now being thrown about or suspended in the cabin void. Some tried to catch others as they were hurled about. The aircraft leveled off from the dive and the fog cleared as quickly as it had arrived.

In spite of the chaos I finally recognized that we must have had a pressurization failure and therefore it was normal procedure for the pilot to descend immediately below 10,000 feet. When sudden loss of pressurization occurs, the suspended moisture in the cabin turns to visible vapor or fog.

The remainder of the trip was pure hell. We were past the point of no return and in the storm for the next couple of hours. Men were throwing up and the smell was getting to me, but the noise from the storm and aircraft was more overwhelming, At least I couldn't hear the gagging going on around me. I was hanging onto a strap like everyone else, hoping it didn't break under the load. I thought to myself, how I would rather take the freezing cold at a higher altitude, anytime, than be in this storm. The "G" forces were so high; I half expected the wings to come off.

When we got to Cubi Point an ambulance was waiting and took a couple of the men off on stretchers. Up to that time, with so much time to think about the dangerous situation we were in, this was the most fearful I had ever been of losing my life. Some of my fear was due to my knowledge of loading and "G" forces and the remainder was of the unknown.

I heard from a couple of the grunts getting off the C-130 that they and others thought there was a fire on board. That would explain why some of the men were trying to get to the ramp door at the back of the airplane. If more men had panicked during the decent, the aircraft could have exceeded its' "Center of Gravity" limit, stalled and crashed into the stormy sea. If I had been in the cockpit and had known what was going on, I probably would have felt better. But, as a passenger, with no control over my situation it was hard to cope.

A stamp was banged into my passport, "Arrived N. A. S. Cubi Pt. (Subic Bay) 20 Dec 1968 and signed by the Control Officer. I made it, but my knees were weak and my ass was numb from the experience!

I'd had enough of Marine transient bunks and was looking forward to a room of my own with peace and quiet; no one snoring, yelling, farting, or, stumbling through the hooch in the middle of the night, stinking drunk. Olongapo is a small village just outside the base perimeter and within walking distance, so my plan was stay there for the night.

By the time we landed and I walked out the main gate with my Marine duffle bag, it was early evening. In the darkness, I was taken aback by the sight of the main street lined with neon lights of all colors. I had forgotten what bright lights were like and couldn't take my eyes from the spectacle. It was one bar or go-go dancing club after the other, as far as I could see. Swabbies (navy personal) were everywhere, with local girls hanging on their arms. Filipino street venders were lined up on both sides of the road. The noise and smoke of the motorcycles was almost unbearable. Yet it was a feast to my sensations. A flurry of motorcycles was weaving their way through the smoky traffic. There seemed to be a total lack of law and order. I was engulfed in another world I wouldn't have believed existed, unless seen with my own eyes.

I was dirty, tired and looked like I came from the war zone; but it didn't deter the girls standing at the bar entrances. I could hardly make my way down the main street without a girl grabbing me on the arm, or other body parts, attempting to get me inside the bar door. Most of them were in scant bikinis and I could see from the entrance, nude girls inside dancing in cages.

The local men spotted my duffle bag and were grabbing me by the arm, trying to take me to a "good, quiet, cheap, hotel!" When I refused, I was promptly asked, "Do you want a number one girl for the night?" When I said: "No thanks", I was quickly asked, "Maybe a young boy?" I kept walking but wasn't sure where I was going. All of the main street bars had rooms above, to go to with the prostitutes. Anyone could rent a room with a girl for an hourly or nightly rate. But that was not what I was looking for. I had a plan to get some rest, catch a bus to Manila and make my connecting flight to Hong Kong the following afternoon.

I made a stop to buy a poncho from a street vender. I wasn't in the mood to bargain and just paid him what I knew to be an inflated price. I was told it could rain without notice in this jungle terrain, plus it could provide me with some warmth if I had to ride in a C-130 again. I made another stop and bought some rice from one of the food vendors. It had what looked like a couple large fried roaches thrown on top. I was told they were "flying rice bugs." They were crunchy but good. It had been about 24 hours since I had eaten, so nothing deterred me at this point and everything smelled great.

I saw an MP on the corner watching all the chaos around us and I asked him where I could get a "quiet room." A big smile appeared on his face and he pointed down the block away from the main street. After all the lights, this street seemed to lead to total blackness; but I saw a rundown hotel on the next corner. At this point I was so tired, I didn't look any further. It wasn't far from the local bus station. All I remember was getting to a dark, single-room, using the bathroom, shared by everyone in the hotel, which had only cold water. It wasn't exactly as I'd planned, in fact it was a noisy restless night and I kept thinking of the early morning bus departure.

I was glad I had the poncho. I walked to the bus station in the tropical rain of the dark morning. This proved to be another first. I could have taken an air-conditioned military bus to Manila, but it departed later in the day and arrived too late for my flight. So, I elected to take a local bus. I boarded the bus trying not to slip in the aisle, on the wet, bare metal floor, covered with clumps of mud. The seat coverings were worn to the extent that springs were sticking from them. I was first on and tried to pick a seat in the middle of the bus without a sharp, broken, spring. I was warned of the bad roads and the rough ride in the back of the bus and thought it not wise to be in the front in case of a head on collision. I couldn't get any of the windows closed and the rain poured in onto the seats and floor. So much for trying to make up for sleep lost the night before.

Even in the darkness, I could see I was the only "round eye" on board. People were getting on with their chickens, goats and pigs. The Filipinos biggest sport was cock fighting so many people had their prize birds with them, in cages, off to Manila to make their fortune at the cockfights.

At daybreak Sunday the bus departed. It was overcrowded and a few men were standing in the aisle. I noticed the bus was full of smiling faces, all trying to get a look at me. I assumed they were amused to see a round eye riding on local transport.

The roads were unpaved and the constant rains kept the roads full of deep, water puddles. Where there were no large holes, the bus driver would increase the speed over the "wash board" roads, to the point that the windows rattled so badly I thought they would break or fall out. I told myself, "I will never complain about another bad road again." The rain stopped and I could see the untouched beauty outside my window. We broke out above the rain clouds into heaven. The single lane road twisted and turned up and down the muddy sides of a tropical rain forest. I could see wild monkeys swinging from the trees in the huge canopy overhead. There were no guardrails on the slippery road and on some curves, I would look out my window, not to see the edge of the road; but the edge of a cliff to the cloud covered jungle below. What an adventure!

It turned out to be five or six hours of being tossed about. I had enough treacherous road adventure for one day and I almost missed my flight from Manila. The bus was late due to the rain and a flat tire that needed to be replaced on the slippery slope of the tropical jungle. Traffic was crazy in Manila and it was a wild ride in the "Jeep-ne" (heavily decorated and brightly painted Jeeps used for taxis) to get me to the airport. By now, I had made my mind up. There was no way I was going to go back to Da Nang via Cubi Point, especially not during the monsoon season. I would spend the money in Hong Kong for a direct flight.

I cleared customs and immigration in Hong Kong on Sunday night, December 21. I wasn't prepared for Hong Kong. What an overwhelming city in size and population! I had been to New York on numerous occasions, but this was mass hysteria. I stayed in a four star hotel on Nathan Road, Kowloon the first night. Kowloon is on the mainland peninsula. The island of Hong Kong was just a ten-minute ferry ride across the bay. My hotel was a five-minute walk from the Kowloon ferry terminal. The Island of Hong Kong was the business center of the country, and the buildings were more modern; larger and taller than the mainland. I wanted to be in the older more traditional area, so Kowloon was my choice to bed down.

Before leaving Marble, I had arranged to meet "Little Don" in Hong Kong. Don was in the same hotel on Nathan Road and his wife was arriving from Ohio to spend the holidays with him. Don and I became good friends over a short time. He was a Tech Rep for North American and based at Marble on a six-month contract. Don had thinning red hair that made him look older than his actual late 30's. His short and thin stature was overshadowed by his overwhelming smile and personality. Don arrived direct from Vietnam, in comfort, on a commercial flight the same night as me. We decided to spend Monday on the town together, before his wife's arrival Tuesday morning.

Don and I went out in the afternoon to look for a bathhouse for a good scrub-down and massage. It was strange to walk down the sidewalks of Kowloon and witness a "sea of black heads" all around me. I was much taller than the Chinese so I could look over the hundreds and hundreds of black heads of those on the sidewalks. Indian tailors were everywhere and would try to coax Don and me into their stores.

Before I departed Nam, I was given a couple of tailor's business cards from Marine buddies that had previously been to Hong Kong on R&R. I wanted to have a couple of good suits and a pair of shoes custom made. I chose one of the cards, feeling I wouldn't get ripped off as much, if I were a referral. Once inside the dimly lit shop, the Indian tailor was very accommodating, pouring me double shots of scotch while I was going through men's fashion magazines. I decided on a double-breasted, black pin striped wool and a three-button sharkskin suit. The double-breasted suit was US$30 and the sharkskin was US$35. By this time, I had a few too many complementary scotch whiskies and the Indian talked me into a dozen monogrammed silk shirts, custom made at US$7 each. Last but not least, he used his silver tongue on my whisky sodden brain to talk me into buying a couple pairs of civvie slacks, for every day use in Vietnam. I felt like an inebriated king.

We found a great place to have a public bath and massage. I hadn't realized how badly the dirt had collected in my pores or how much dead skin I had. After a very hot soaking bath, the masseur rubbed a towel over my skin in a long stroking action. Large rolls of dead skin peeled from my body. After the scrub, cold beer was served during the rubdown. I thought I was in heaven.

After feeling like I had been given a new body, Don and I were back out on the streets again looking for a place to have dinner. We were looking for something special and decided on a place the masseurs at the bathhouse highly recommended.

Once inside the restaurant we were told the specialty of the house was "Peking Duck" and was not to be missed. The waiter proudly brought the duck to the table for us to examine, before it was prepared. It was truly an all night feasting affair. I cannot remember how many courses we had; maybe five or more, ending with soup. After each course we had a tall bottle of local beer to refresh our palate while waiting for the next course to arrive. What an experience for my taste buds and worth every Hong Kong dollar.

After dinner, Don and I decided to go straight back to the hotel to get some much needed sleep. By now, I felt like I was stuffed and squeezed like a sausage into my new skin. Back at the hotel lobby, Don and I were waiting for the elevator to take us up to our room when two lovely Chinese girls walked up to us and tucked their arm inside ours. We were asked with a big smile, "Would you like us to sleep with you tonight?" The elevator arrived and the doors closed without us entering. Don and I just looked at each other and smiled. Before we could say anything they told us the price would be US$15. They were strikingly beautiful and reeked of heavy sensual perfume.

Initially, I was aware of the increase in my heart rate and felt overwhelmed by their approach and offer. Slowly engaging my common sense through my alcohol-saturated brain, I knew all the excitement over the last couple days was enough and quickly, but kindly, rejected their tempting offer. Don was also impressed with the girls but followed my lead. The girls were polite about the rejection, but stood with us arm in arm, for a couple more minutes in a last desperate effort.

Realizing we were not going to change our minds, they retreated to one of the sofas in the lobby. We no sooner punched the button for the elevator again, than a female came running through the lobby calling Don by name. Don turned and ran directly into her waiting arms. It was his wife. She had arrived on an earlier flight than planned. Don introduced her to me and quickly went to retrieve her bags.

I'll never forget the look on his face. Don was aware that if his wife had arrived a minute earlier, their reunion might not have been so happy. It would have been difficult to explain why he was standing at the elevator door, waiting to go up with a girl on his arm!

The following morning I found another place in Kowloon within my price range. It was directly across the road from my hotel and called the Chung King Mansions. It was in an old high-rise building above an arcade of shops. One complete upper level of the building was owned and run by a local Chinese family. I had a quiet comfortable room with a bath and breakfast was served every morning at a large communal table. The owners' family and children ate at the same sitting and treated me like family. The only rule was, "No prostitutes in the room." This was a home with a rule I could easily keep. I loved it.

I found myself walking almost all day from street to street. Then at night I'd walk more. It was great to walk freely without danger. There were a couple of streets in the bowels of the dirty city, where all the bars and clubs were located. As I was walking down one of these streets passing the girls standing at the bar doors, one approached me from behind. She had silky white skin with black hair and looked like model material. "Where are you going?" she said. I replied: "Just walking and enjoying the sights." "Come back to the bar and buy me drink", she said with a big smile on her lovely face.

I just returned the smile and kept walking. Now, walking down the sidewalk, beside me she asked, "What's your name?" I said without thinking, "Dick." She started laughing and pulling at my arm. I stopped and looked at her. "What's so funny?" Your name is not really Dick, is it?" I felt a little confused but answered, "Yes!" She stopped laughing long enough to say: "OK, I'll call you Dick and you call me Pussy!" I finally got it, and started laughing along with her, then I made a final statement, "I'm just out for the night air, but thanks anyway."

She finally gave up and made an about turn to her post. I could still hear her laughing as she shuffled down the sidewalk. I had been using my nickname all my life without ever thinking of the connotation. From then on, I started introducing myself as Richard to women.

I returned to the tailor two days later for a second fitting of the roughly stitched together material. At the end of the week I went in for my final fitting. I had never had a piece of clothing fit me so well. I packed everything I bought, except for a couple of the white shirts and the slacks, and shipped them back to Pennsylvania.

After the sight seeing, the good cheap food, lovely ladies and the bright lights, I was rested and ready for the flight "home." Since it was the holiday season, I found it impossible to obtain a direct flight from Hong Kong to Saigon without going through Manila. The Manila to Saigon departure was 6:00am on New Years Day, so I made the decision to take a flight from Hong Kong to Manila on New Years Eve, over night, then catch the 6:00am flight out of Manila.

But the best made plans don't always work. A well- known quote I like to use is, "If you have time to spare, go by air!" I arrived at the Hong Kong airport for my late afternoon flight. I cleared immigration and found that the flight was going to be delayed, for some unknown reason. We waited for a few hours then the officials decided to take us back out of the holding pen, through immigration to eat at the airport restaurant.

I had hoped to have a nice meal in the Carlton Hotel Restaurant in Manila to celebrate New Years Eve, but my hopes were dashed. At almost midnight, we were processed through immigration again. Stone sober, I watched the clock on the holding pen wall strike midnight. All was quiet in the room of tired and frustrated passengers.

Our flight finally departed at 3:00am and by now I had lost all hope of catching the morning flight from Manila to Saigon.

When I finally arrived in Manila, I found that all flights were booked up for a week. I had to get back to Marble as soon as possible, so I made my way back to Cubi Point and got on the C-130 manifest on January 3 to Da Nang. I'd sworn I wouldn't do that, but when you're desperate, you'll do almost anything. Fortunately, all went well. The flight was uneventful and I was able to stay warm enough in my new poncho!

It was actually a good feeling when I landed at Marble. It seemed like I had been away much longer than I had. Marble was feeling like my real and only home and I must say, I missed my friends. I only had a little over three months to go now till I returned to the real World.

I was starting to have mixed emotions about leaving the beauty and excitement of Vietnam. I had a beautiful sandy beach 100 yards from my hooch, was fed well, had cheap drinks and was free to do almost anything I wished. What more could any one ask for? We were even organizing to have our own shower, with hot water, built onto our hooch. My biggest problem was that my hormones were rushing and I was having a hard time keeping them under control with the temptation constantly around me.

Chapter 10
Back to Reality

I was given two pieces of bad news my first day back. I found that Stubbs was killed the day after he took me to Da Nang. He was on a sortie in an OV-10 and the aircraft was in a target dive. He never pulled out of the dive and the aircraft exploded on impact. Either Stubbs suffered from target affixation or got hit with ground fire. The grunts found his remains and his AO, in a shallow grave a couple days after the crash. Someone who found Stubbs said that it looked like he was used for target practice. I was angry and in shock at the same time.

My second bit of bad news was; that they couldn't find a replacement for me at the end of my six month contract, so I had to stay another six months; one year! Is this what I really wanted? Did I enjoy it that much? Was I trying to hide from what I had to eventually face when I went back to my family? I had it pretty good in my position. Many a Marine had to spend a year in Nam, under a hell of a lot worse conditions, but now I had over nine months to go!

Life went on while I was away. Ack was quite angry and wanted to go home. He still had about three months to go, but was very worried about the actions of his wife. He showed me a photo of his wife with a Christmas present she bought for herself. She was covered with a, full length, mink coat. It appeared his wife had been on a spending spree with the money Ack was sending home to save for a rainy day. He was also worried about her tone of voice in the tapes. It sounded like she had enough of the marriage and was going out to all the local nightclubs. Ack was livid and constantly paced the floor. I knew he was worried, because he was spending little time in bed reading.

While I was in Hong Kong, Joe and Jack went to the Philippines for a week and did some shopping. They bought a quick recovery water heater and a hand basin. The bathroom and shower were about to become a reality. Joe and Jack did all the necessary planning. The water tower seemed to be the biggest problem. Somewhere, somehow, Joe found a water tower, not in use on the base. We bought it with a couple bottles of whiskey and gave the crane driver a couple more to deliver it and stand it up at the back of our hooch. The wood, purchased from Marine supplies, a plumber, an electrician, and necessary supplies were all paid for with whiskey.

The hooch members all pitched in and built the enclosed bathroom. A backhoe was brought in to dig a hole for the septic tank. In about two weeks we were ready to have the water tower filled.

An arrangement was made to have the Marine that delivered water for the mess hall and other shower block water towers, to pass by our tower once a week. And once a week we would have a bottle of whiskey waiting for him.

This was the life. We didn't have to go to the public showers again. We had clean hot showers with a proper drainage system and a hand basin and a mirror to use while shaving.

The next thing I knew it was January 20, 1969, my birthday. With all this shit going on in Vietnam, I was trying to figure out why people couldn't accept one another's values, religions or beliefs without trying to force others to except theirs. Yes, protect yourself and your family from aggression, but otherwise leave them alone. That's the conclusion I was coming to. I was now 29 years of age and didn't think much about living to see my 30th. I took it day by day and enjoyed what I had!

My hooch mates had a little party for me at 161 Rocket Avenue that night. I just wanted a low profile celebration sharing a couple bottles of Chianti and Mateus Rose with a couple of my close friends. That was exactly what I got as well as a big hangover the next day.

A couple of days later I was walking around in the flight revetment area of Marble. Small tractors would be used to transport flat bed trailers loaded with rockets. The rockets were stacked on the 5 x 6 feet flat bed and stayed in place only due to their own weight. I observed one of the drivers taking a corner around the revetment very fast, about fifteen feet in front of me. He was going so fast, that the tractor was now on two wheels. When this occurred, all the rockets on the flat bed started falling out, rolling and bouncing in my direction. One just missed hitting me at ankle level as another bounced by me just missing my right leg at knee level.

The young Marine stopped the erratically moving tractor and got off. He looked my way, gave me a sheepish smile, loaded up his scattered cargo, about fifteen rockets and powered off again. I stood there in amazement. I was thrilled one didn't hit me. I wasn't angry, just thankful.

I knew nothing about what can or can't set the rockets off, but for some reason I didn't consider the thought of getting blown up, until later when telling Jack about the incident. "Ignorance is bliss", as one famous ignorant person stated and lived to tell the tale.

Chapter 11
TET

The monsoon rains and the cold weather became more evident as winter set in. At night the temperatures would occasionally dip into the 30's (F), with blowing rain for days on end. While at Marble, during one period it rained for 18 days straight with only short intermissions between downpours. One non-stop session of rain lasted for five days. During that time, rain was recorded at 22 inches in 24 hours and the following day at 26 inches in 24 hours. None of us had ever experienced anything like that before. It was a good thing that the base was on the beach and most of the water ran off into the South China Sea.

After the first night of drenching rain I got up in the morning to make my routine visit to the six-holer, to find it floating in the middle of a large pond of water. We were amazed to find most of the others floated away also and I had to join a long line waiting in the pounding cold rain for one of the few still in operation. There were some anxious moments that morning and for a few days to follow as half the base didn't have six-holers in operation. The pissers were nowhere to be seen as they were overflowing and surrounded by a perimeter of water.

The humidity was 100% and tempers among the troops wore thinner by the day. There were many more fights than usual. In fact I had a drunken maintenance sergeant pick a fight with me in the flight hangar during one of those rainy days. Fortunately I was able to talk him down and cool his temper. I made it clear that he was going to get hurt and after getting out of the hospital end up in the brig for fighting and being drunk on duty. He lost the respect of his men that day which was a sad thing. A couple of days later, after he sobered up, he apologized to me for his actions, but it didn't slow his alcohol consumption.

During the day, flight line maintenance was at a minimum. There was never enough room in the dry hangars for all the work to be performed. Therefore, because engine changes and keeping the aircraft in flight condition was essential, the work was continued in the revetments. We used rain ponchos during the first couple of days of heavy rain, but after a short time, I realized, along with everyone else, we were better off without ponchos. It was difficult to work with them hanging over our arms and found they were extremely hot in the middle of the day. Because of the high humidity, I would be just as wet under the poncho from dripping perspiration, not to mention the smell of the ripe bacteria from the previous days of wear.

I endured the elements while riding the Honda on the road to Da Nang one rainy day toward the end of the eighteen-day deluge. I had to get off the base, if only for a couple of hours. On my way north on Highway One, I saw the effects of the flooding on the huts in the small villages. The built up road I was riding on allowed me passage over the sea of water on both sides of the road. In the huts with no doors or windows, I could see families in their typical native squatting position only visible from the waist up. Didn't they have enough sense to move from their flooded house? What arrangements were made for cooking and sleeping? There were probably no options for these people, except to stay, wait it out, and protect their hut and only possessions.

As I drove on I reached a small bridge crossing over a normally lazy creek and found the bridge under a torrent of water. This made it impossible to go on and I had to turn back to the base.

Nothing much was flying during those days. We paid dearly for it when the rains let up. Charlie had taken advantage of the bad weather by using water buffalo to move their rockets and mortars into strategic positions around the base. Chinese New Year, known as Tet, was now upon us. Charlie was always most aggressive during the week leading up to the celebrations; it was the worst time for conflict. Nothing was different this year and all hell broke loose, as expected.

One night I was caught off guard at Marble. A couple of mortars came in and everyone in the hooch ran to our trusty bunker after the first one. I was in bed and sound asleep without a stir when a rocket came in close by. That "crack" must have jolted me out of bed, but I wasn't awake yet. I was standing at the screened front door with my eyes open, when another rocket came in and landed about 20 yards in front of me. The flash and loud concussion in the soft sand brought me alive with adrenaline.

Without thinking, feeling the concussion, I spun around to run to the trap door. I was off balance and fell over, with my forehead striking the corner of my steel bed frame. I was stunned, but I got up and made a mad dash for the bunker. When I got there, all eyes were on me. I was covered in blood. It was running down the left side of my face and I was puffing like hell from the excitement. Everyone thought I got hit with a piece of shrapnel and were all over me until I told what had happened. They started laughing their asses off. I was still a little dazed and didn't see the humor until later.

The next morning, I wandered out to inspect the damage from the rocket. I found a couple of holes in the front of our hooch and a piece of shrapnel in my bedside clothes closet that was leaning against the same wall. I went across the road from our hooch to see the six-foot deep and fifteen to 20 foot wide gaping hole in the sand to bear witness of the rocket impact.

The following night, Charlie didn't even wait until we went to bed. At about 10:00 PM, without warning, a rocket came in and shook our hooch. It didn't take me long to get in the bunker with the others. We looked at each other and I said: "That was too close!"

Soon after, another two rockets came in, but further away. Then quiet….. We came out of the bunker wondering where the rockets landed.

I walked out the front door of the hooch onto Rocket Ave. In the dark of night, I could see people running back and forth in front of the parked emergency vehicle lights. I ran up Rocket Ave. to see men frantically digging through the remains of smoldering hooch, looking for survivors. I was told there were six men in the hooch at the time of a direct hit. No one was alive.

The hooch next to it was ironically, a Casualty Receiving Area. Two injured men in casualty were in beds against the wall adjacent to the destroyed hooch. They were blown out of their beds, but not seriously injured.

The following morning I walked up Rocket Avenue to the destroyed hooch to witness the damage and take a couple of pictures.

The rescue workers were still looking for body parts in the rubble. I could see the anguish on the faces of the six or so Marines who were carefully lifting the pieces of twisted metal and splintered two by fours. I watched for a while in silence…… I couldn't help feeling sorry for the families of the men killed in this hooch and wondered if any of the corpses would be recognizable when the body bags were handed over to their loved ones. I took a few pictures, and moved on to the flight line to pursue my daily rituals.

Some of the 122 mm Rocket Damage Caused at MMAF

Six men were killed in this hooch the night before; men now gathering body pieces.

The morning after a night of "incomming"; fire truck had a near direct hit to it.

****

Jack, Ack and I were due for another trip to Da Nang. On a bright sunny Sunday morning we talked Jerry into taking the Jeep. I was riding in the back with Ack and Jack was riding shotgun. The serene streets were almost empty and it was nice to get off the base. I could check out the sights better from where I was sitting, than on my Honda. Jerry slammed on the brakes narrowly missing an RVN soldier darting out from the right side, directly in our path. His arms were in the air frantically swinging his rifle. Still alarmed by the confrontation, we heard rifle fire ringing out to our left at 10:00 then to our right at 2:00. The lonely RVN quickly took cover behind the Jeep and it didn't take us long to take cover beside him. The RVN friendlies were firing across the street about 20 yards from us, at VC returning fire. The VC were on the opposite side of the street, shooting from the windows and doors of the buildings. If the friendly RVN had not jumped out to stop us we would have been caught directly in the crossfire.

A two or three minute firefight occurred with us lying on the dirty street in no man's land. It was like watching an exciting panoramic stage play from a front row seat. I didn't feel like we were in any danger, I only felt the rush of pure exhilaration. The VC were concentrating entirely on the return fire of the RVN. The firefight ended as quickly as it started when the VC seemed to evaporate inside the scarred bullet-riddled buildings.

I realized as the ordeal came to an end, I had my 45cal in my hand but didn't fire a shot. I was prepared to do so, if the RVN retreated and left us behind. A 45caliber pistol is only good for close range, but it would stop a charging man in his tracks and I would fire only if I had a good target in range. A couple of minutes later the RVN crossed to the left side of the street in a shooting-frenzy but drew no return fire. All was quiet now and we decided we had had enough excitement for the day. We filled the seats of the Jeep and went back to Marble. Jerry wouldn't go to town any more, not even on his motorcycle.

I was about due for another day in Da Nang, to have a change of pace. On the last visit, the week before, we ended up in the middle of the firefight and missed the chance to have a chat with the girls. So, I made my usual trip around the familiar market places and by late afternoon, I stopped into my favorite bar. After a couple of beers and a chat with the giggling girls, it was time to hit the road back to Marble before the curfew. I wasn't going to take the chance trying to get out of the city encompassed with barbed wire and untrustworthy RVN.

One of the bar girls, Kim, asked me for a ride home because the bar was about to close and her ride did not show up. Kim said she lived in a little village "just off the road" on my way. I reluctantly agreed, but I felt like I was doing her a favor. She side straddled my running Honda and we were on our way just before dusk. Heading south on Highway One, my passenger gave me instructions where to turn off to her village. After about five or ten minutes, I had to slow down to negotiate a path between the rice paddies, usually used by buffalos and bicycles. I turned on my headlight, because it was getting too dark to see the trail. By this time I was wondering if I would be able to find my way back to Highway One.

I stopped the Honda as we approached the path leading into the jungle and told her: "I'm not going any further, you can get off and walk from here." Kim insisted, "Not far now, just ahead." I drove on, questioning my sanity. Another couple of minutes passed; more turns in the heavy growth and we came out of the jungle into the secluded village. In the darkness, the native kids came running alongside of me as I pulled up to her thatched house.

I was trying to keep the kids from climbing up on the Honda when Kim told me to come inside and meet her family. "It's too late to go back to the base and too dangerous in the dark!" she said. Considering the position I was in, I decided to stay the night. Kim instructed me to bring the Honda into the hut. "It would be safer", she said.

As I was pushing my Honda through the entrance to the hut, I could hardly see what was inside the dimly lit room. I was aware of two tatami mats on the bare ground with just enough room between to park the Honda. To the left and right side of the entrance wall were a couple of chairs. Once I put the bike on the center stand, I turned to see two Vietnamese men sitting in chairs and a slender young Vietnamese woman standing beside them. Kim introduced the young lady as her sister. Turning to one of the seated men with only a sarong wrapped around his body, she said: "This is my brother." The brother gave me direct eye contact and a big smile. The man sitting next to him was in some kind of uniform and was cleaning a watch with a rag. "This is my sister's boyfriend, he is going to stay overnight also." She went on to say: "He and my sister will sleep in this bed", pointing to the tatami on the left side of the Honda, "You and I will sleep on the other tatami on the other side."

The boyfriend didn't raise his head from the watch cleaning or acknowledge the introduction. I could now see by his stature that he was not as slender as a typical South Vietnamese man and his uniform was not of an RVN. In the dim lighting I tried to study him a little closer. As my eyes focused, I make out a holstered pistol on his right side. My conclusion was he was a hardcore NVA soldier.

Not quite knowing what to do next, I unzipped my light jacket enough to reveal my 45cal shoulder holster. Kim looked at me, seeing that I was annoyed and uneasy about the "boyfriend." With a smile she said: "It will be OK, there will be no trouble."

Just then a mama san stepped into the hut with a naked toddler straddling her hip. Kim introduced her mother. Mama San gave me a big smile as Kim said something further to her in Vietnamese. I could see the black betel nut-coated teeth and some of the juice running down her chin. The mama san pointed to her daughter's boyfriend and said to me: "Him VC!" She was on the verge of laughing,...... then still smiling, she turned and quickly disappeared from the crowded room, taking the child with her. I could feel my knees go weak and my blood run cold before my adrenaline kicked in.

Without further delay, I told Kim: "I'm going!" Kim tried to reassure me that it would be all right. "Stay,... no go", she kept saying. I could tell she was visibly upset with me for not wanting to stay the night.

How could I sleep with the enemy in the bed next to me holding a loaded gun? It would be a long night and maybe before morning, one of us would be dead. I didn't want it to be me. I didn't like my odds and thought it safer to get the hell out of there. I was faced with trying to watch my back while backing the Honda outside the hut. I kept thinking of how to drop the Honda and get the 45 from my holster to fire, if he started for his gun. I wondered if he would attack me with his skilled martial arts. He still didn't pay any attention to me and continued his watch cleaning. Hopefully he was worried as much as I was. Maybe he was only interested in a romp on the tatami with Kim's sister?

I didn't take my eyes from him and managed to get the Honda outside, even with Kim's distracting desperate chatter. Now outside, I was faced with kick-starting the Honda and getting clear of the village children without getting shot in the back. I assumed that he had a rifle or AK-47 somewhere in the hut. Thankfully the Honda started with one kick and in one motion it was in gear and I was off. Fortunately, the village children did not have enough time to hear the Honda running to investigate and impede my retreat. Lying down on the gas tank, leaving a trail of dust and in total darkness without lights, I sped off waiting for a bullet to find me. Fortunately, there was none.

I had to find my way back to the base, so I turned my headlight on to see the narrow jungle track. I had been running on pure adrenaline but the effects were starting to wear off. I couldn't think and I found myself shaking so badly that I had to stop on the trail to regain my composure. It was time to get my head straight and concentrate on finding my way to the base. I turned my lights off but didn't kill the engine.

I didn't want to stop but I had to. I realized that the engine noise from the Honda would soon attract any unfriendlies in the area. I turned my lights back on and forced myself to move on. I came out of the heavy growth and experienced a dark moon-less situation. With my dim headlight, I could only see the narrow path that lay in front of me. I knew the rice paddies had to be on each side of me, but I couldn't see anything in the black voids. Trying to keep one eye on the stars, I was twisting and turning on the dikes of the rice paddies, but was still trying to continue in the same easterly heading. It seemed endless with me being the only person in the wilderness. I had to be careful not to run off the dirt track, as I would end up in a rice paddy. I kept thinking about how I got in this predicament and was whipping myself for it. But now wasn't the time to think of anything else except survival. I have no idea how long I was riding around in the dark.

To my amazement the dirt track finally ended. At first I was shocked, but soon I realized that somehow I managed to find Highway One by a different track than the one I went in on. I could have jumped off the Honda and kissed the paved two lane road, but I wasn't home yet.

I made a right hand turn onto the hard surface and headed south to Marble. My head was down and the throttle was against the hard stop. Even if someone did shoot at me, I wouldn't have heard it due to the noise from the redlined 90cc engine.

When I approached the Main Gate, I turned the headlight off, and slowed to a halt. I yelled out in the strongest American accent that I could, "Don't shoot, I'm an American!" A Marine answered, "Advance and be recognized!" I dismounted the Honda and with one hand in the air, slowly walked it up to the barbed wire stretched in front of the locked chain linked gate. I could see on both sides of the gate, sandbagged machine gun bunkers. The guns were all pointed at me and a bright spotlight was put into my face. One Marine said: "What the hell are you doing out here after curfew and where's your ID?" I didn't go into the specific events that had led up to this, except for saying, "I got delayed in Da Nang" while holding my ID up like a badge of honor. The gate opened and the barbed wire pulled aside for me to ride in. I can't express the relief I felt to be on safe ground; or at least out of pistol or rifle range for the night.

****

At Marble one evening a couple of weeks later, I was draining my bladder at the pisser outside our hooch. As I stood there looking out at the dark sky, it seemed to be more quiet than normal. Then a bright spot appeared on the horizon. As I watched, it started growing in size and brightness at an alarming rate. I couldn't believe my eyes and stood in amazement. Then I saw something I had never seen before. Even in the night sky, I could see enormous waves of sound come towards me, like a large boulder was thrown into a still pond. The fireball grew to an alarming size and it took about two or three seconds for my senses to warn me of the impending danger. I threw myself to the ground not knowing the effects of the visible shock wave. I felt the concussion on my body and the deafening booming drum effect from every hooch and metal building on the base. The echo throughout the base set off the incoming sirens. I lifted my head out of the sand to see the ball of flame appearing like an intense sunrise, right on my doorstep.

Realizing the immediate danger had passed I got up and ran to the hooch to get my camera and tell the others. The hooch had been evacuated and everyone was in the bunker. I yelled through the open trap door into the tunnel. "Come outside and look at these explosions." Everyone was yelling back to me, "Get your ass in the bunker before you get killed!" I grabbed my camera and went back outside. Large explosions were still occurring one right after another. The secondary explosions were nowhere the size of the initial one, but large enough to be able to rattle the sheet metal hooches. After about 10 minutes of taking pictures, the explosions were still going on but not as intense. I ran back inside the hooch to see why no one else was out there with me. I found them still inside the bunker and I started laughing like hell because I was convinced there was no danger from incoming. They finally came outside for a quick peek, then went back to the safety of the bunkered hooch. The hooch rattled and boomed all night from the explosions, making it difficult to sleep, even for me. Jerry and Ack slept in the bunker that night. General consensus was that a big VC offensive was going on and the base might be over run by Sapper squads at any time.

At sunrise, I woke up to hear the explosions still going on. I got up to find the out what happened. At morning chow I was told that a U.S. cargo ship, while docked at Da Nang harbor was blown up by a direct rocket hit from Charlie. The ship was loaded with explosives, ammo, and 500 lb. bombs that were due to be unloaded this morning.

I had to see the ship or what was remaining of it with my own eyes, but I had to wait another day for the explosions to stop. I got on my Honda with my camera strapped to me and headed north on Highway One. The road was thick with tanks and armored vehicles. Everyone was on full alert. There was a roadblock about 300 yards from the explosion site, but I managed to get through it with no problems.

When I got closer, I could see the bow of the ship resting completely out of the water about 30 yards from the docking area. The remainder of the ship was blown into small bits and scattered over the water and surrounding area Tanks on the docks were blown onto their sides and tops like toys in a kid's sand box. Unrecognizable debris, unexploded bombs and live rounds of ammo were scattered everywhere. Some of the military barracks that had lined the dock were flattened to the ground. In the distance I could see damage to standing barracks almost a quarter a mile away. One hell of a mess! I could not imagine how many lives were lost in this one hit. I took some pictures and went back to Marble in disgust and asked myself more questions like what the hell are we doing here and why doesn't the U.S. government let us win the war? Why don't we go into the North and take it over? Why can't we stop this screwing around with "police action"?

I read in the Stars and Stripes newspaper a couple of days later that fifteen men were killed in the explosion at Da Nang Harbor! There was no mention of the collateral damage. It would have been funny if it wasn't so serious. If I hadn't seen it with my own eyes, I wouldn't have known any better. But as it looked to me, at least 100 or more were killed. The propaganda machine was alive and well and I wanted to scream, Bullshit!

Action on the Western Perimeter at MMAF

Top: Note the OV-10 on the left getting ready for a sortie

Ammo dump was exploding and out of control for days.

US Navy Ship blown out of Danang Harbor

Piece of ship's bow (left), and progressive damage to the hooches from the blast

Tanks and crane damaged like toys. Note an unexploded bomb, bottom left.

Chapter 12
Shit Happens

A couple weeks after the attack of the ship at Da Nang Harbor, it was back to business as usual. It was time to make another trip up country to the DMZ. I planned to make a day trip directly to Dong Ha, take care of inventory, assess damage and return to Quang Tri for the night.

By now Don Schmitt, another Garrett Rep, was positioned in Quang Tri to support the T76 engines. Don was heaven sent for me. I managed to convince headquarters to provide another contract to cover the northern sector. It made my job much easier, as I knew Don very well and he could be relied on. Don Shmitt, Rick Colrick and I started to work for Garrett AiResearch on the same day. Rick's badge number was 9921, mine was 9922 and Don's was 9923. We would always kid each other about who had the most company seniority. I was the youngest. Don had about four years in the Air Force and worked in General Aviation before he was hired at Garrett, while Rick, the oldest, in his late-thirties, had been in supervision for the General Electric Engine Division. What experience Don did not have in turbine engines, he made up for with his knowledge of aircraft and ingenuity.

We spent the first three months together in Phoenix during our initial training. The three of us stayed at the Gaylord Motel on Vanburen Street. After a long day at classes the three of us began a ritual. We would change into our swimsuits and meet at the pool for some sun and a beer. When the sun was weak in the sky we would meet at one of our rooms to study for an hour or so. Then we were off to dinner and later stop at a bar for a Coors draft. I must say, we really got to know one another through and through by living in such conditions. We all had the same work values, sense of humor, and looked out after one another. We were all married, although Don and Rick more happily. Little did Don and I know at the time that Rick was earmarked to be the head of the T76 field service department at Phoenix and both of us would be indirectly reporting to him.

I was looking forward to seeing how Don was doing in Quang Tri within his new assignment, having a couple beers with him and talking about "The Real World." I heard through the grapevine that he had fit right in and made friends quickly with one of the Maintenance Sergeants.

When I arrived at the Marble Mountain Air Field helicopter pad that morning I saw a familiar face. Henry was a civilian GE Rep that was staying at Marble in the hooch next to mine. He was making his way to Dong Ha also. The last time I'd seen Henry was a couple of nights ago on my way back to my hooch from the O club. I heard a groaning noise and caught sight of a man's figure lying face down looking as if he was suffocating in the soft sand. In the moonlight I could see his head desperately trying to move from side to side struggling to get air. I quickly lifted his head from the sand, expecting the worst. I rolled him over thinking he had been shot or stabbed. I recognized Henry, even in the dim light. He was still gasping for air and moaning helplessly but he didn't seem to have any obvious wounds.

When someone else arrived at the scene, we carried him to his hooch about 40 yards away. His hooch mates rushed to the door to assist him to his bed. They were really pissed off. It appeared that someone had spiked his orange juice and he was allergic to alcohol. This wasn't the only time that someone had a good time at Henry's misfortune, but it almost killed him that night. One of his colleagues went to fetch medical attention and I went to my hooch thinking how lucky it was that I just happened along. He didn't know that I helped him that evening. He was a good-looking man in his early thirties, married, with a young baby. I remember being glad that he would see his baby grow up.

It wasn't long until a CH-46 Sea Knight landed for refueling and off-loaded some hard core grunts covered with mud and sweat stained clothing. They looked like they had been in the jungle and rice paddies for quite some time. They had blank looks on their young faces as they came down the rear-loading ramp in the whine and rotor noise of the chopper. As soon as they off-loaded, another platoon climbed aboard and took their position on the long webbed seating. I went to the cockpit and asked where they were going. He informed me by pointing to his chart, moving from Marble Mountain and ending at Dong Ha. I was in luck, but as usual, I had no idea what stops he would make in route.

A new procedure had been put into place. Each passenger had to put his name and destination on a manifest. This list or manifest would remain behind with one of the ground crew on the fueling pad. Henry and I did this then took a seat beside the grunts and the loading ramp was closed by one of the two ships gunners. With a teeth-jarring thump and shudder from the rotating blades we were off and away, heading north.

As usual the wind was blowing through the window openings and everyone in the chopper sat quietly in the deafening noise with rounds of ammo protruding from our ears. This time I could see that we were not going over Hai Van Pass. When we got to Da Nang Harbor we followed it out to the South China Sea. With the mainland on the horizon behind us, I could see that we were approaching a large hospital ship. The red medical cross was readily visible on the side and bridge of the ship and I could see a helicopter-landing pad in view. The Sea Knight shuddered over the pad then landed. The ramp was dropped and a small, insulated box was given to someone waiting at the end of the ramp. As soon as that person cleared the pad with the box, collective was pulled, the Sea Knight again shuddered heavily and we were off again.

I had heard rumors that there was a hospital ship off shore used entirely for treating and experimenting with "infectious incurable diseases." It was rumored that when someone got crotch rot, VD or something doctors couldn't cure or control, they were taken to this hospital ship. They were kept in isolation and weren't allowed to return to the U.S. until they were cured. Seeing the ship confirmed the rumors, and gave me another reason to keep "it" in my pants.

We continued our flight maintaining about 200 feet. Flying above the beach with the jungle canopy at the edge was a fantastic sight. Once again, it reminded me of what a paradise this place really was.

Eventually we turned left from the beach, tracking a course for Quang Tri and soon made our final approach to land on the refueling pad. When approaching the pad at about 40 feet altitude, at the end of the revetments I could plainly see someone in an OV-10 on the run up pad, running both engines. Someone else was standing outside the aircraft with his fingers in his ears. I knew that the majority of the time the OV's were on the run up ramp if they had just installed an engine or if there were problems with one.

Once on the pad I decided to run back the 50 yards to where the engine runs were being carried out, to see if I could give any assistance. I knew if it was an engine problem that required more than a few hours of troubleshooting the engine would be quickly replaced to keep the aircraft in an airworthy condition. I didn't want that to happen. If Don wasn't aware of it, or in the immediate area, the maintenance crew would waste no time consulting him before they replaced the engine.

It was a low torque problem, a grounding item, so I decided to stay and assist. A few more minutes went by and I could see the Sea Knight lifting from the pad in a storm of sand created by the wash of the rotor blades. I watched the Sea Knight heading north and thought how unlucky I was to miss that flight. This would probably stop me from getting to Dong Ha and back to Quang Tri by this evening. But with any luck staying to assist would save an engine replacement and the shipping back and forth of it to Marble for repair. I was fortunate enough to identify a torque pressure shift. Within an hour we had made the necessary readjustments and released the aircraft for flight.

Shortly after Don made an appearance, walking down the PSP full of smiles. He had been at noon chow. It was great seeing him looking so happy and enjoying what he was doing. Everyone on the line had great respect for him. I knew I didn't have enough time to take care of business in Dong Ha, so I decided to stay the night at Quang Tri and leave tomorrow.

That night Don, Michael Bell and I went to the Officers Club for a couple of drinks. I was surprised to find that Don was drinking very heavily. It wasn't like him. By the time the evening was over, he had a skin full and was on his ass. When we got him back to the Tiltin Hiltin, Don was crying. Michael told me that Don was drinking like this every night. Sobbing, Don told me that he didn't want to end up like his father. He went on to say, that his father was an alcoholic and he had lived in an abusive situation. His dad died at an early age and they were never close.

After about an hour of talking, Don passed out on his bunk and I went off to my bunk for some much needed rest. I knew I had another long, hot and dirty day ahead of me but I couldn't sleep well that night thinking about Don and what he was going through. The isolation of Quang Tri was having a detrimental effect on his physical and mental health and I felt helpless to do anything for my close friend.

The next morning, I was off to Dong Ha. When I got there, I was told that yesterday had been a really bad day. Heavy casualties from rocket and mortar attacks and a couple of aircraft were damaged by incoming. "There was a full scale battle going on yesterday", said one of the hardcore grunts. It sounded like it was a good thing I wasn't there. I took my notes, gathered information and hoped to catch the next chopper back to Qunag Tri, but there were no flights going the remainder of the day. All the choppers were being used to haul the grunts in and out of a position known as the "Rock Pile." There was still a lot of activity and fighting and they anticipated a big hit on the base that night.

I wanted to get the hell out of there. Knowing that Quang Tri was about ten miles as the crow flies, I made a quick calculation and came to the conclusion I could walk it in around three hours. I had very little gear to carry because I didn't plan to stay over night. It was still early enough in the afternoon to have time to walk all the way, but I counted on getting a ride on the road by hitch hiking.

As I cleared the main gate I could see that everyone was in the "full alert" position. Grunts were in their heavily fortified bunkers with weapons pointed to the defoliated open outer perimeter. I must have looked ridiculous strolling out the gate without any protection except for my shouldered 45cal.

As I walked down the dusty road, occasionally a couple of tanks or armored vehicles would pass me by. I stuck my thumb out but they just left me behind in a cloud of dust. There was not a local anywhere to be seen. Not even a mama san. But, I felt as long as there was traffic headed south I'd be safe. If all the traffic was headed north or back to Dong Ha, I might be in trouble.

After about an hour, I saw a lot of ground and flight activity off to my right. It looked to be about 2 miles away. Marine Broncos were dive bombing and dropping white phosphorus. Shortly after, an F-4 Phantom made a quick pass over and dropped napalm on the marked position. I had seen napalm dropped while I was in the air, at a safe distance, but seeing it from the ground was much more than breathtaking. The ground shook under my feet and I could feel the added heat and smell the fuel in the air from the napalm. It was a little too close for comfort and the pucker factor was increasing. I kept telling myself that at least the snoop and poop wasn't in front of me.

Almost running now, I tried to get the action behind me. More tanks headed south but no one would pick me up. I was getting a little anxious about my decision to walk; but I kept trying to convince myself I wasn't in any immediate danger!

Then out of the blue came a jeep with a Marine Captain behind the wheel. I stuck my thumb out and he swerved just in front of me and came to an abrupt stop. I ran up to the jeep as he was backing up to meet me. He was armed to the hilt. Helmet, flack jacket, 38cal shoulder holster, hand grenades, cartridge belt full of ammo, holstered 45cal and an M-16 snapped in the dash for easy access and good looks. The look on his face would have shattered a 20-pound. steel ball. Snarling, he said to me, "What the fuck are you doing out here?" Before I could answer he ordered, "Get the fuck in!" He didn't have to say it twice. I said to him: "I'm headed for Quang Tri, are you going that far?" With another quick look at me and with eyebrows raised like he was going to kill me, he replied: "You're in luck you dumb fuck!" The Captain had a way of expressing his feelings and looked like he would make a good "lifer".

Speeding down Highway One, our Jeep would approach a tank with a trail of dust behind it and the next thing I knew we were in the passing lane going around it. The aggressive Captain was driving blind not knowing if anything was coming the other way or how many tanks he had to pass. He was driving like a maniac and I started to think I would have been safer if he hadn't picked me up. Fortunately the road was straight. There was no further conversation between us. I didn't want to say anything to him that would take his mind off the driving.

I guess it wasn't my time to die. He dropped me off just inside the gate at Quang Tri. I got out and thanked him. He just gave me that "you dumb fucker" look and he was off again maybe to save another "dumb fuck" like me!

I got back to the Tiltin Hiltin and headed for a shower straight away. I had to get the dust off my brown face and body. I dreaded to think how much dust I had inhaled on the road today. After my shower I waited for Don and Michael so we could go to early evening chow. I was even hungry enough to eat the crap that was served at Quang Tri and grateful I wasn't out there with the grunts trying to hold the line at Dong Ha. To me it was worth the adventure to get back here for the night.

At the O Club that night, I promised myself that I would have one drink then go back to the hooch and get some sleep. I wanted to make an early morning departure for Marble. The chances are always better then and I didn't want to get stuck along the way in some "arm pit" of a place en route.

Don, Walt and I bought a drink from the crowded bar and while walking to a table, a tear gas canister was thrown into the middle of the floor. Everyone started running for the doors, choking and yelling. Fortunately we were close by an exit and made a quick dash for it. I hardly got a whiff of the tear gas before I was outside. Don and Walt were right behind me and weren't effected either. There were still more men behind struggling to exits gasping for air. I thought we were under attack but soon found that some "asshole", one of the Marine's finest, set it off just for a joke. Some joke! A number of the officers were knocked to the ground during the mass exodus and suffered injuries from being stomped on.

"I'm going to bed", I said to Don and Walt. Don said he was going to one of his buddies' hooch to have a couple of drinks before turning in. Walt was sitting on his bunk trying to read a book in the dim light when I fell asleep. However I awoke suddenly in the middle of the night when all hell broke loose. A couple of rockets came in and I heard M-16 fire and machine gun fire very close to our hooch. I could also detect AK-47 fire. AK's have a sound all their own and it is easy to detect the difference from the American M-16's. That meant Charlie was breathing down our necks.

The next thing I knew, the Marines were yelling that we were being over run from the river perimeter and to take cover. I didn't feel safe running outside to the bunker and just laid on the floor in the hooch. I figured my chances were better inside than running outside and having some Marine taking pop shots at me thinking I might be Charlie. I had an M-16 beside my bed and quickly grabbed it. It was dark as hell with the power cut and Walt and Don were nowhere to be seen. I called out for them but had no reply. The next familiar sound was a Cobra Helicopter flying almost directly overhead before it started firing rockets from its' pods. The impact explosions were only a short distance away and I could see the flashes through the cracks of the vibrating corrugated sheeting of the hooch wall. Then came the bruup, bruup, from the Cobra gattling guns. I kept my position on the floor in the dark hooch next to the bunkered wall. Other explosions were going off, but not as close as before. I kept waiting for someone to run into the hooch and I was ready. After about half an hour, the shooting stopped and I could hear Marines passing outside the hooch door yelling, "**all clear**."

After a while Walt strolled back to the hooch from the protection of the bunker and Don arrived somewhat later; drunk but none the worse for wear. He had still been drinking at his buddies' when the action started. Sappers had broken through the river perimeter with satchel charges, firing AK-47s. They had not made it as far as the flight line but managed to carry and throw a couple of charges into the bunkers about 40 yards from our hooch.

I never did find out if any of our men were killed. The number of causalities seemed to be secret unless you personally knew those who were killed or injured. It was hard to tell how many Sappers got through the lines, but as far as I was concerned, it was one too many.

The next morning, I had early chow with Walt and headed for the transient pad. I boarded a CH-46 bound for Marble. It was loaded to the gills with hardcore grunts and gear on the floor extending right to the end of rear door ramp. I assumed a position on the right hand seat toward the back and close to the ramp. When the ramp closed, I noticed a couple of grunts climb onto the sea bags and gear stacked on the ramp door, to lie down. It was a cold, and misty morning. I was having a hard time keeping warm with the cold damp wind blowing back through the open window ports in front of me.

The pilot was flying at about 1000 feet and it looked like we were at cloud base. We headed due south, then changed course in a southeasterly direction to head for the beach. I figured the pilot was unable to go over the mountain range to the south of us at Hai Van Pass due to cloud cover, so we would track down the beach to get around the mountains. When we got to the beach line we were down to about 400 feet above the ground and the clouds were just above us. After a couple of minutes the pilot had dropped the chopper down to about 100 feet to stay under the clouds.

Five minutes passed and all of a sudden it was a **white out;** "zero visibility." The helicopter came to a sudden stop and maintained a hover position. In doing so the pilot pulled a couple of "G's." I looked toward the cockpit then outside to see what the pilot was going to do. Out of the corner of my eye, I saw that the rear ramp door had fallen open and all the stacked gear was falling out. Then it hit me, "Where the hell were the grunts that were lying at the door." It appeared they had fallen out with the gear. While still in the white out, the pilot maintained his altitude and position while one of the aircraft gunners ran over the gear on the floor to quickly close the door with the hydraulic selector valve. I tried to tell him that there were a couple of grunts on the door when it opened, but there was so much aircraft noise that he couldn't hear what I was saying and I couldn't hear him. The gunner talked to the pilot on the intercom, and after about a minute, the pilot turned back north again until the white out disappeared.

I thought we were going to land on the beach and start looking for the missing grunts. We turned 180 degrees to the south again and dropped down to where the jungle canopy on my right was higher than my line of vision. The rotor wash from the chopper blades was now blowing a cloud of sand around us, making it impossible to see the beach. The next thing I knew, the pilot started gaining forward air speed and kept going at 10 or 20 feet above the beach. "What the hell is going on? Aren't we going to look for the grunts?" I was yelling to the gunner. He just shook his head with a blank look.

The next thing I thought about was getting out of this chopper alive. I watched the jungle on my right passing in a blur with little or no visibility. Was the pilot crazy? What the hell could he see in front of him? Was he watching the tree line on the right side and just keeping it within his vision? What if someone else was doing the same thing coming the other way? I kept waiting for the moment when we would hit a tree with a rotor blade, or impact with another object. I had a bad feeling about this. This hadn't been a good trip and maybe my luck had run out. After what seemed like an endless black hole, we broke out of the fog into clear skies. I looked around and saw smiles on the mud-covered faces of the grunts.

All the trash or low cloud cover must have been contained on the north side of the mountain range. The pilot must have known this, but as far as I was concerned, he took too much of a risk. I also wondered about the grunts that had fallen out and would they send a rescue party? When we landed at Marble, I asked one of the grunts about the missing men, "We lost some gear, but no men" the grunt said with a smile. Apparently when the door started to fall open the grunts jumped off the door onto the cabin floor, just in time.

What a week, I thought. Now safely back home, I dropped my gear on my bunk at 161 Rocket Avenue, I felt like I had been through a war! It was almost noon and I had just enough time to take a quick shower in clean, hot water before noon chow. My hooch mates would be arriving shortly and it was nice to be alone for a short while to reflect on the events.

After my shower, I lay on my bunk and thought how nice it was at Marble. It was good to be back. I heard motorcycles stop in front and Jack, Ack, and Jerry walked in. They looked at me like I was a ghost. Each one came over and hugged me. I couldn't figure out what was going on. "What's the joke?" I said. They quickly told me: "everyone thought you were dead!" I knew by the way they looked and how they were talking, it was true.

The smiles had dropped from their faces. Looking very serious, they went on to ask, "weren't you on the Sea Knight going to Dong Ha with Henry?" Feeling puzzled, I answered, "yes!" Then Jack said "Well………. it was hit by ground fire and brought down about 3 miles north of Quang Tri. Everyone on board was killed!" There was a long silence as I tried to grasp what I was being told. It wouldn't register. It was like I was in overload and the words were just running off without being absorbed. They went on to tell me, "U.S. military headquarters informed Washington D.C. and it was passed on to Garrett in Phoenix. They have listed you as missing in action, until they are able to identify your body. The chopper burned on impact and it was almost impossible to identify anyone, or even know how many bodies there were. All they had to go on were the names listed on the manifest of those who boarded the chopper at Marble bound for Dong Ha. Yours was on it!"

Henry was dead. The chopper must have been hit shortly after I watched it flying off. If I had watched it any longer, I might have seen it go down with my own eyes. Maybe it was for the best, not to see it go in. I thought to myself, "Why didn't I find out sooner?" It had been almost three days since the accident. Apparently too much action was going on in Quang Tri and Dong Ha.

There were heavy casualties and they were still trying to confirm the body count. No one else knew that I got off the ill fated Dong Ha flight and no one I'd met in the last two days knew my name was on the manifest left behind at Marble.

My mind raced with all that had happened and then I had to "take care of business." First I had to tell the base commander. I was relieved to find that my family had not yet been informed that I was missing in action; but the Government would have done so by the end of the day.

What a twist of fate! I was alive and Henry was dead. He was to live only a couple of days after I lifted his head from the smothering sand. I guess he was destined to die. Suddenly I wasn't worried about dying. No point, I reasoned, when death knocks at the door, I'll be ready. I don't have a choice. Sooner or later "something" is going to get me. I couldn't give a shit even less!

Chapter 13:
Desperation vrs The Good Life

Ling was one of the local Vietnamese girls serving drinks in the Officers Club. She was very attractive and showed quite an interest in me. She was well mannered and well dressed, either in traditional or western clothes. She wouldn't put up with anybody trying to manhandle her while she was serving drinks. I had noticed more and more in the last couple of weeks that Ling was trying to catch my eye and give me a flirting smile every time she came near.

One night Ling came to my table and whispered in my ear, "I would like you to come to my house sometime "for lunch"! At first I couldn't believe I heard her correctly. But after Ling walked back to the bar to pick up a couple more drinks, she turned and gave me the warmest smile. I knew I heard her correctly. I was blown away, but could not refuse the offer. After all it was "just lunch"! To go off the base and meet a lovely local lady that wasn't a prostitute for a lunch was like a fairy tale. Maybe I could find out how the other half lived. Ling and the other waitresses were not allowed to fraternize with anyone on the base and would get fired if found out. Discretely, over the course of the evening, we made plans; we set the date, time and she provided me with a "mud map" to get to her home in Da Nang City.

We made plans for Sunday and the closer it got the more nervous I became. Had I made the right decision to meet this lovely lady? I had been in Vietnam too long and my hormones were rushing after seven months or more of abstaining. What was this going to lead to?

I still had a family and I didn't want to get involved with another women. Other men I knew had been involved in long-term relationships with local women and found it extremely difficult to go back to the real world. I decided to make this a "lunch only" and enjoy the day with a local lady who could readily converse in English.

The Saturday night before our scheduled rendezvous, Marble was extremely active. The base was hit with rockets and mortars all through the rainy night with a couple of sappers over running the western perimeter. I couldn't sleep thinking about my Sunday lunch. All this other shit was getting me down. At chow that morning the place was buzzing. Things hadn't gone well through the night because we couldn't use any air power to hold our lines. It seemed like the VC were building up more and more in under ground tunnels off to our west from where they were able to come out at will. Meanwhile many of the Marines were getting letters from back home with news of the anti-war rallies growing by the day. The frustration among the Marines seemed to be worse than ever. All the bombing in North Vietnam and on the Ho Chi Min Trail didn't seem to make any difference at all. The VC seemed to be getting stronger and I couldn't understand why we weren't allowed to overrun North

Vietnam and put a finish to all of this senseless killing rather than just trying to hold back the inevitable tide of infiltration. Laos and Cambodia were attempting to be neutral in the war, but the Ho Chi Min Trail funneled south within their borders to South Vietnam. The U.S. took a stance as to not have official active resistance within those two bordering countries, but "unofficially" the CIA was heavily involved in Laos and Cambodia. The CIA enjoyed full support from the Thai Government. Thailand was a staging point for the CIA operation. CIA aircraft and arms could be moved into Laos and Cambodia from the northern borders of Thailand. But with all this "police action" everything seemed to be coming apart at the seams.

My thoughts jumped back and forth; one minute thinking about the serious political implications of what was happening around me, and the next about my lunch date with a beautiful lady. I was ready to escape from reality and get on my Honda and ride. As I was getting on my bike, Jack and Ack tried to persuade me not to leave the base. I just gave them a smile as I kick-started the Honda and headed down the wet road, in the light rain with my poncho flapping behind me. I was told before my departure that the main gate and the western perimeter were currently secure. Once again it took some persuasion to get through the main gate. Ironic that this time I was trying to get out and not enter! Once I cleared the main gate there were numerous tanks and armored cars lined all the way up Highway One. Some parked in defiance and some were moving to or from position. Unlike my experience at Dong Ha, I had transportation and knew the road like the back of my hand. As I was passing one of the tanks on my way north, I suddenly realized the rear of the tank track was coming right for me. The driver in the tank didn't know that I was passing him and decided to make a turn off the road. The pivot action kicked the aft end of the rotating tank track well out into my line of travel, almost wiping me out. It all happened so fast, I didn't have time to take evasive action. The track just missed me and I learned a lesson without getting hurt. Keep well away from a moving tank.

By the time I got to town it was pissing down rain and it was difficult to find Ling's place. There were no street signs and my only reference was the rain soaked mud map that she had provided.

Determined, I found her small apartment at the end of a very narrow alleyway in a derelict building. Ling greeted me at her door with a big smile and a look of excitement. She said: "I didn't think you would come." "Da Nang suffered from rocket and mortar attacks last night with a lot of small arms fire on the streets." In the confines of her small but well kept western style apartment was a toddler. The little girl was introduced as her daughter. She had a lovely face with a mix of western features.

"Will you sit down and have a beer", she asked? Then she apologized for not having much to offer for lunch as the morning markets were closed due to all the rocket activity. I was somewhat disappointed but managed to say softly, "It doesn't matter." Underneath I was thinking how I was looking forward to a traditional Vietnamese lunch. "But", she said: "I've made noodle soup. It's not much, but it will be hot on this cold day." I found Ling very kind and thoughtful, smiling through it all. As I was drinking my beer, she was telling me about her boyfriend and her life. While she was talking she was trying to keep the toddler on a "short leash", but she was very loving in her actions. I was thinking to myself how courageous un-resentful she was.

While eating, she continued to tell me about her boyfriend, the father of her child. He was a Canadian civilian and lived with her for over two years. His tour was up and he was recalled back to Canada. He had been supporting her after his return by sending her "some" money to help pay the bills. She explained that he was trying to get reassigned to Vietnam, but to no avail. It had been nine months to a year since his departure and Ling was starting to feel desperate. I began to wonder where this was going to end! Why did she invite me here? Was this a "sting?"

The next thing I knew, she brought out all her monthly bills and budget. "This is what it costs me to live". Ling started to go over the details, when I decided to speak. "So what are you asking of me?" I said. She looked at me like I should have known and said: "I want you to move in with me and be my boyfriend." I realized then that she didn't want a handout or a one-night stand, but a long-term relationship with someone that would pay the expenses. This was not just a lunch but also a proposal.

I was embarrassed. I really felt sorry for her, but I couldn't see myself moving into another family. Even though I wasn't happy in my marriage, doing this would only screw my mind up even more. Ling was beautiful and I was impressed that she asked me to share her life, but I couldn't do it. It was hard to look her in the eyes and say no. The smile dropped from her face and tears started to form in her eyes.

I wanted to get out of there. I felt guilty and truly unhappy about her unfortunate circumstance, it had taken great courage to ask this of me, I offered her $20 in MPC. As I handed her the money she took a small step back and said: "I'm not a prostitute and I cannot take your money"! "Well, let me pay you for the lunch, that's only fair" I said and placed $10 on her table.

As I walked from her apartment I turned, waved and said "Bye-Bye" to the little girl who was smiling happily and still waving, in contrast to the flood of tears now streaming down Ling's cheeks. I was almost sick to my stomach. I was feeling hopelessly sad and Ling had touched me in a way I had never experienced before. I wanted to help her and make her smile the way she did when I first walked into her apartment, but I couldn't. I had my own family to think about.

Ling at the "O" Club

There was a sudden change in the air. Spring came and along with May, Easter had arrived. To make life interesting, our hooch gave a bottle of whiskey to one of the cooks in return for a couple dozen fresh eggs. We didn't have any food coloring to brighten up the eggs, so we had to improvise. We hard boiled the eggs then used a black marker to write some of the sayings that were heard around the hooch at night. Some of them being, "I want to get laid", "Peace Sucks", "Mattress back Ack", "Fuck You Ack", Straight Arrow Dick", "I'm Horny" and "Fuck it I'm Short!" To be "short" meant your tour of duty was almost finished. We had a few laughs that Easter Sunday and drank a few bottles beer and wine. We all sat on the back porch of our hooch in silence that night and watched the sunset.

It was warming up and the South China Sea was calming down with the waves becoming flatter each day. During my daily run on the beach, the onshore breezes didn't have the cutting, damp cold I had noticed just a few weeks before. I could almost smell the change and it was good to be alive.

I made friends with a Sergeant, a native Hawaiian by the name of Sammy. He asked me one day if I wanted to go spear fishing with him on Sunday. Sammy had arranged a boat with an outboard engine to get out to the reef just off China Beach where Charlie's Navy could be frequently seen on the horizon, fishing. Before going, we made some hand slings from surgical cord obtained from the base hospital. We were going to spear rock lobster.

When Sunday arrived it was a beautiful sunny day with no wind. Sammy and two other Marines piled into the boat after we pushed it off the sandy beach. "This was the life." We each had our M-16s with us in case Charlie had other ideas about us being out in their fishing area. We arrived at a spot that was crystal clear; the coral bottom no more than 15 to 20 feet below the surface. Once out there we could see there were about 20 to 30 of Charlie's Navy boats around us. We decided on an anchorage that was at least 50 yards from the nearest fisherman. We could see them standing in their dish shaped boats casting hand nets overboard and pulling them back in.

Once our anchor was set, it was decided that two of us would stay on board and watch Charlie. The two Marines decided they would be more comfortable remaining on board assuming guard duty and not diving as originally planned. We presumed Charlie would keep their distance, especially if they saw two round eyes standing guard with M-16s in their hands. Sammy and I were over the side. Sammy was able to obtain a couple of facemasks and snorkels. This was the first time in my life I had experienced diving on a coral bed and I was overjoyed. I completely forgot about where I was or the danger I might be in. All I could do was dive to the bottom and look at the array of tropical fish and beautiful soft and hard corals. I longed for a set of gills or to have the lung capacity of a turtle. After numerous trips from the surface to the bottom, I spotted a lobster peering out from under the coral. I was just about out of air so I made a quick return to the surface, got a deep breath and went back for the kill. It was easy with the sling spear and I brought my catch back to the boat with a big smile wrapped around my snorkel. Then I was told that Sammy had already speared about six or seven of them while I was off with the fairies in La La Land.

Back on the bottom again, a deafening sound come from my right side and almost made me gasp a lung full of water. I struggled quickly to the surface not knowing what to expect. I could see the two Marines firing their M-16s in the direction of one of Charlie's boats. I realized I wasn't hearing the gunfire, only a loud ringing in my ears. "What the hell is going on", I thought. The Marines were motioning for me to get on board and I could now see Sammy right beside me. While one Marine was helping Sam and I get into the boat, the other was still firing his weapon. Once on board, I could see he was firing over their heads in attempt to chase them away. I was still in shock from the blast in the water.

Our engine was started, the anchor quickly retrieved and we were out of there. After we were back on shore a couple of hours the ringing started to subside and my hearing started to improve. I then found out that while Sammy and I were under the water, one of Charlie's Navy threw a hand grenade into the water to stun or kill the fish. The fish would float to the surface after the concussion and the fisherman would throw a net over his catch. The Marines were only trying to scare him off by firing over the fisherman's head.

We had a "cook out" Hawaiian style that night. Sammy was one hell of a cook. He made a wood and charcoal fire behind his hooch in a 55-gallon drum. We were able to obtain steaks other food and condiments from the mess hall and with our fresh catch the four of us drank whiskey and feasted like kings.

Afterward, we laughed and drank more whiskey with beer chasers. Ling came to my mind during the evening. The alcohol effects drowned out the pain I felt when I last saw her, and I forgot about where I was for a few precious hours. The alcohol was giving me a better view of my life also. I started to appreciate that I had a good life with very few problems relative to others deprived by humanity.

My ears continued to ring from the under water concussion for the next few weeks, but it was all worthwhile.

Chapter 14
Changing of Personnel

Jack and Ack were disappointed. Their replacements should have arrived. Both were running over their 6 months contract, but replacements were difficult to find. No one wanted to go to the war zone and resisted right to the point of being fired from AiResearch/Garrett. So of course Jack was grinning from ear to ear when a Garrett Rep replacement walked through the front door of our hooch. Jack got to go back to the "land of the big PX" in the next day or so. Ack was to stay on a couple of weeks and overlap with the new guy. I knew in advance that there would be no follow on contract for Jacks' position on the flight line, so Ack's replacement would be responsible for the CER shop and the flight line. There were so many protests going on in the U.S. and around the world, the word was going around that it looked like the U.S. was going to start gearing down the military commitment little by little. The plan was to allow the RVN militarily to take full control of their country.

I was really sad to see Jack go but happy for him at the same time. Ack was fun to have around for a laugh, but Jack Norton and I became real and lasting friends. In a few weeks Ack was going back to a broken marriage, and Jack was going back to a very understanding and devoted wife.

George Handley was a Garrett Rep whom I'd never met before but his reputation preceded him. One look at him and the smell of the alcohol in his sweat sodden Hawaiian shirt confirmed the story. George was a middle aged man, known for being a two fisted drinker. I didn't want him, but Rick Colerick told me that they couldn't get anyone else to fill the slot. George had been thrown out of the last couple of assignments in the U.S., due to his drinking or tardiness and was informed that this was his last chance. But as I saw it, the war zone was not a place to send an alcoholic.

George had bought into Jacks' hooch area. We had moved George in the night before and Jack stayed in the transient hooch for his last night before departure. We had a big night at the O club that evening to celebrate Jack going home. George was drinking two or three to everyone else's one. At .25 cents for a double scotch it was like he died and went to heaven. The following morning I had one hell of a time getting him out of bed. When he finally put his feet on the floor he reached for the bottle of scotch at his bedside and poured a water glass, almost full. He sat there and drank it, almost without taking a breath. I stood in amazement. He finally got up and started bitching, "I didn't want to come here." I told Rick Colerick before I departed Phoenix that, "I will stay drunk the whole time I'm here." Rick told him if he didn't go he would lose his job. Since George had a wife and family to support, that wasn't an option. This gave me a good indication of what I was going to be up against. What a hell of a way to start the first day of his new assignment.

After seeing Jack off, Ack and I took George out to the Engine Shop and Flight Line. I could tell George wasn't interested and the Marines could detect his attitude straight away. After a couple of hours in the mid morning heat, he reeked of alcohol. He was covered with perspiration and wanted to go back to the hooch. Ack was worried because he wanted to leave as planned. I took George back to the hooch hoping he would sleep it off.

That night after chow, George got his second wind and went back to the O Club for another drinking bout. By the time he got back to the hooch it was well after midnight. George was drunk out of his mind and had picked up a couple of other drunken buddies. It was bad enough with Jerry, but now George as well!

The next thing I knew he had nailed a cardboard silhouette of a man at the back door of the hooch and started throwing knives at it from the front door. Right down through the middle of the hooch this knife would fly on its way to its' target. What the fuck? Drunks throwing knifes, laughing and still chugging drinks down between the throws. Someone was going to get hurt. I got out of my bunk and started raising hell. I chased the other two drunks off by almost throwing them out the door. George started to threaten me with his knife. He was so drunk I just took it from him. Hardly able to stand, he yelled and threatened me for a couple more minutes before settling down to bed.

What next, I thought? I decided to wait a couple more days and see if I could get him to straighten up. I wanted to see the back-side of Ack on his way to the World. He had lost all interest in what was going on around him and was almost paranoid about getting shot or blown up before his departure. His mind was on his unstable marriage and what awaited him on his return. He came to Vietnam thinking he would go back with a little extra cash in the bank, but now was facing the fact that he would probably lose everything including his family.

The next morning when I left the hooch, George was still in bed snoring. He never showed up for duty that morning. When I got back to the hooch at midday, he was gone and I didn't see him till that evening at the O Club. At the Club, George was standing on one of the tables yelling and acting like a drunken fool. The officers were trying to get him down and calm him, but he kept resisting and threatening. I didn't want to be associated with him and kept my distance. If he got his ass kicked, it was his problem. When he arrived back at the hooch that night, it was the same all over again, except this time I didn't wait. I stopped it before the second round of knifes were thrown. I had a plan. I rushed to the back door and grabbed the knifes before they could get to them. Now I was in control. I chased his drunken buddies off and told George to go to bed. With a snarl and evil eyes, George said coldly: "You'll pay for this!"

The following day, the men on the line were all talking about the new civilian from Garrett. I felt very concerned for Ack and decided to go to the Base Commander for a consultation. He made a phone call to Phoenix to have

George replaced as soon as possible. I wasn't worried about Crazy George face to face, but sleeping next to the asshole was a big worry to me. I didn't want to wake up with a knife sticking in me; anyway, I didn't trust him.

To avoid confrontation, the Base Commander decided that I should make a trip up country that afternoon and he would call George in and tell him the bad news; he would be packed up and gone before I returned from my trip.

A week later I came back from the trip to find George gone and Ack still there. With wide eyes Ack told me about the nightmare of the ordeal that he had faced. The afternoon George was informed by the Base Commander that he was to get on the next flight to Phoenix, the shit hit the fan. The Commander did not tell George how the decision was determined, but George had a strong suspicion that I was the instigator. George immediately started trying to find out where I was and was telling everyone that he was going to kill me.

Ack was to personally make sure that George caught the flight the following morning from Da Nang to stateside. Apparently George didn't sleep at all that night. He spent the night in the hooch drinking, throwing his knife and waiting for me to walk in the door. Ack said: "The later it got, the drunker and more angry he became." When Ack put him on the plane the next morning, George was quoted as saying; "I'm going to kill that bastard, when he gets back stateside." "He's ruined my life and he's going to die for it! I'll find him and cut him wide open with this knife." That gave me a warm all over feeling. George was crazy enough to do just that!

A couple of days later, Ack's contract was cancelled! With Jack and Ack's contracts cancelled there would be no T76 engine Reps to support the CER shop or the Marble flight line. If only I had known this was coming! I would have let George stay on, Ack go home and the position would have been canceled without me being responsible for having George fired. They were canceling contracts right and left. By now the Marines were well trained up on the T76 engine and the Bronco.

Ack was thrilled to go home. The war was over for him, but he had to deal with a wife that wanted a divorce. Ack felt sure that his wife had spent all the money he was hoping to have saved.

Jewel Langford was a slim man in his early twenties, and a Garrett engine logistics person from Phoenix. He was a little naive and had been brought into the 1st MAW at Marble to help straighten out the parts situation. He was a whiz when it came to engine parts and was desperately needed. At times the Marines had to steal parts from the Air Force warehouse at Da Nang Main, just to get aircraft back in the air. AOG's were a big problem due to the lack of parts.

Jewel bought Jacks hooch space and Honda after George got the axe. He had a six-month contract and it looked like he would beat me back to the Real World. As Jewel was single, good looking, with dark skin and coal black hair, the girls in the Officers Club all fell in love with him.

It wasn't long until one of the single girls in the club talked him into moving in with her in downtown Da Nang. We all tried to talk him out of it, but he was in love! He had already given her money to rent a place and buy furniture for the love nest. He had seen the apartment and thought she spent the money wisely but in the end, he decided to keep his bunk in the hooch to stay on occasion or if things didn't go well.

The last afternoon before his move, Jewel was nothing but smiles. Friday afternoon had arrived and he was going to be at his apartment before curfew, spend the weekend and then be back on Monday morning for work. He was really looking forward for some time in the sack with his new girlfriend. Off he went on his Honda. As we waved good-bye I yelled at him, "keep your pecker up and your head down!"

That night at Marble was a bad one. We had incoming rockets and mortars almost all night. Jewel was back in the hooch shortly after sunrise the next morning. He had lost his dark complexion and was as white as a ghost. "What the hell are you doing here at this time of the morning?" Did you forget something", I asked? I had never seen Jewel lost of words before. He simply walked straight to his area, undressed and crawled into his bunk.

When I finally got up for Saturday morning chow, Jewel was still sleeping. When I got back from chow, he was just getting out of bed. He looked like death warmed over. He was still sitting on the edge of his bunk with his head propped in his hands. Jerry had just walked out of his cubicle still smelling of alcohol from the night before, also to find out what happened. I asked, "Are you OK Jewel?" He didn't look up and was still holding his head and looking at the floor as he blurted out, "I'm never going back there again. First, there were incoming rockets and we had no place to go but under the bed. Then there was a fire fight right outside our apartment, men were banging on our door wanting to get in, followed by more shooting outside I am lucky to be alive! I'm never going back there again!"

Without hesitation Jerry looked down at Jewel and said: "But did you get laid?" That was to be expected of Jerry, but I couldn't help breaking into a laugh. Jewel was silent and couldn't see the humor in Jerry's question.

Jewel didn't go back, except to pick up the things he left behind. In fact he didn't leave the base much after that. I knew he really had the shit scared out of him and he was never the same old Jewel again.

I made good friends with a Gunny Sergeant everyone called, in a respectful way, "The Chicken Killer" The Gunny got his name one day when he charged a VC hut under heavy fire.

As the story goes, there was a wounded Grunt on the ground close to the hut and the Gunny tried to rescue him. The Gunny was unable to get close to the wounded Marine and in trying to do so, caught a round in his arm.

Now the Gunny is pissed off and with his M16 blazing he charged and ran inside the hut. Dozens of chickens started flying out the windows and doors, then all went quiet. After a minute of silence the other grunts thought he might have been killed in the hail of bullets. But out of the hut door the Gunny appeared, M16 in his right hand, one dead VC tucked under his left arm and a dead chicken hanging from his left hand.

The Gunny had saved countless men from Charlie during medivac missions. He didn't consider his own safety when there was a wounded Grunt on the ground or in some rice paddy. I had a lot of respect for him. Everyone did!

The Chicken Killer had offered to give me one of a dozen tomato plants that he had been growing in five-gallon cans beside his hooch. I asked Jewel if he would give me a ride on his Honda to pick the plant up after evening chow. He agreed, and when we got to the Gunny's hooch, the Chicken Killer wanted us to stay and join a beer party with a few of his close friends. We were quick to oblige and a couple hours later left for our hooch.

Jewel kick-started the Honda, I got on behind and the Gunny lifted the five-gallon potted tomato onto the small luggage rack behind me. With both of my arms strained behind my back I was just able to hold onto the precariously perched drum. All the men from the party were out on the road to see us off. They were laughing at the sight of us. Everyone had too much to drink.

The Marines were yelling, "let's see you do a wheelie, Jewel!" I was quick to say, "Forget it Jewel!" He replied loudly: "Nah, I'm not that crazy." When he started pulling out slowly in first gear I felt relieved, but all of a sudden he laid into the throttle then popped it into second gear. All I could see was the back of Jewel's head and the night sky ahead of him. Holding the pot was impossible, because now the bike was almost vertical. Somehow I managed to slide off to one side of Jewel and the motorcycle before the impact.

I went down on the road and skidded on my back to a stop, fortunately only experiencing some "Honda rash."

Jewel wasn't so lucky. He fell to his back, on the road and the motorcycle continued running on top of him. I jumped up and with the help of the others, removed the motorcycle. He lay there in agonizing pain, his leg broken in the accident. By the time an ambulance came to take him to the base hospital, everyone was sober. The motorcycle only had a couple of scratches but the tomato plant was a write off.

****

Don Naugle had been a Garrett rep assigned to the Air Force at Da Nang Main. Every time I went to 1st MAW Headquarters there, I made a special effort to visit him. He was born in Canada and worked as an instructor for Pratt and Whitney prior to being hired by Garrett AiResearch. He took the assignment because he needed the money badly. His wife suffered from rheumatoid arthritis and had already undergone numerous operations on her hands and feet and still urgently needed a couple more. The increased income for Don was needed desperately. With the 25% increase for "overseas assignment" and 50% increase for "hazardous duty " combined with the $12 per-diem, it was almost double our salary. No wonder the Marines called us Mercenaries.

Naugle ended up being a bit of a problem for me but I really liked him. One day, just before his replacement, he and I rode into Da Nang City for a couple of drinks. He had his own Honda but had never been in town before. Don Schmitt was visiting from Quang Tri and was riding pinion with me. The three of us spent a couple of hours in a bar and then Schmitt and I decided to take a ride and visit the local markets. Naugle wanted to stay behind and have another beer and chat-up the girls. He encouraged us to go without him and we arranged to meet back at the bar at 5:00 Pm when it closed. So off we went.

After checking out the locals and looking at the plastic junk for sale, it was time for Schmitt and me to head back to meet Naugle. I didn't want to be late, as we didn't have much time before curfew. When we arrived, much to our surprise the bar was closed and it wasn't even five o'clock. No one was around the entrance and the streets were empty. I thought Naugle might have decided to hit another bar and come back to meet us at the agreed time. So Schmitt and I waited and waited, but when he hadn't showed by 5:30, we felt pretty desperate. Not only was it getting dark but also there wasn't a soul to be seen on the street. It looked like a ghost town. I didn't have a vague idea about where to start searching for him. We thought maybe he decided to go home with one of the girls; but we couldn't figure out why he hadn't he waited to tell us what his intentions were.

Finally, we couldn't wait any longer. We were about to start the Honda and get the hell out of there, when about four RVN in uniform came around the corner and spotted us sitting on the bike. Two of them lowered their weapons on us and I didn't move a muscle. They walked up to us, still keeping us in their sights and one of them said: "What you do here?"

I quickly replied: "Waiting for a friend."

His response was: "**Di Di Mau!**"

That was one thing I understood in Vietnamese. It meant, "Go!" Now! I'd heard many stories of how unscrupulous the RVN could be. Stories of Americans shot in the back, with their money stolen and the entire thing blamed on Charlie. With our backs exposed I knew that we would be at risk during our departure on the Honda. With Schmitt behind me, I knew that he would get it first!

Off we went, down the deserted street. Just into second gear, I suddenly decided to turn right at the corner to limit the time they would have to aim and shoot. Once around the corner and in the cover of the buildings I experienced great relief that no shots had been fired! I took a left at the next corner and without warning, found barbed wire stretched across the street with armed RVN sentries on both sides, pointing their rifles directly at us and yelling loudly, **"Dung Lai**. I came to a screeching halt, raised my arms and assuming that Schmitt was doing likewise. I didn't even give the guards a chance to say anything before I said loudly, "Marines, Marble Mountain!"

To my surprise it was as if I had just given one of the guards a direct order; he ran over, grabbed an end of the wire and pulled it back far enough for me to pass. I quickly drove through the maze and we were off into the darkness. Again we were an extremely vulnerable position and open to a couple of rounds in the back. The RVN could just say, "It was after curfew and the Americans tried to overrun the barricade." Of course they could also have claimed that there was no money on the bodies when they were searched! But once again there was no gunfire.

Now clear of the City limits, we made our way south, down Highway One. When we were about a half-mile north of MMAB main gate, I notice more flares in the sky than normal. I knew the gate would be closed, so well before our arrival I started yelling, "I'm an American, I'm an American". When I stopped in front of the gate, I thought we were going to get massacred. There were shadows everywhere from the grunts and everyone with weapons pointed at us. It was very unnerving.

One of the grunts yelled out, "What the hell do you think you're doing?"

I told them to open the gate and let us in but someone yelled back from the shadows that they had instructions not to open the gate for anything or anyone. "Our perimeter is currently under attack a couple hundred yards just to the south of us and Sappers are trying to get through the line," they yelled.

They repeated that they could not open the gate and were told to get out. Then I heard some small arms fire in the direction the grunt indicated.

Still, I refused to go. I yelled back, "Get clearance to let us in." Finally the grunt saw that I was not going to leave, and began cranking the field phone in his hand. When he put the phone to his ear, he looked pretty desperate. It appeared he was calling to get advice on how to handle the situation.

At last, he put the phone down, ran to the gate and unlocked it. I could see now that he was a Sergeant and he yelled in an anxious voice, "Get the hell in here!" I didn't hesitate a moment. The remaining guards were looking at us in amazement, I started the Honda again and did a wheelie down the road with Schmitt hanging on for dear life. When we returned to the safety of our hooch all our friends were in the bunker waiting nervously for the ever-persistent Sappers. I discovered later that a couple Sappers did break through the perimeter but were killed before they could do any damage.

I don't know what really happened to Naugle that night. He told me that he decided to head back to Da Nang Main early. But he had this worried twitch when he said it and he was nervously puffing on his cigarette. The twinkle in his eye and that wide smile on his face told me there was another reason. I said: "I hope she was worth it Mr. Don Naugle, but Schmitt and I were left hanging in the lurch." Nothing more was said. Thankfully, there was no harm done to any of us.

A few days later I got a message from the Base Commander that Don Naugle was being held in Saigon, under house arrest by the Vietnamese. He was not allowed to make his scheduled departure from Tan Son Nhut. After hours of frustration and coordination, I was able to speak to Naugle on the landline phone. He sounded desperate at the end of the patched and re-patched phone connection. Naugle explained that the South Vietnamese Immigration would not allow him to leave the country until he paid his Vietnamese income taxes. To make matters even more complicated immigration had confiscated his passport. Americans civilians were exempt from paying local taxes, but since Naugle still carried a Canadian passport; he was required to pay a 60% tax.

At first I didn't know what to say. I knew Garrett would not assume any responsibility for foreign taxes and Naugle did not have that much money because of the burden of his wife's medical bills.

I was afraid that I was going to lose the phone connection, so I told Naugle: "Get your passport back! tell them that you spoke to your supervisor and found that your contract has been extended for another month or two. What ever you have to do, get your passport in your hand and get your ass back to Marble."

A couple of days later Naugle walked into my hooch with a worried smile on his face, puffing on a crumpled and sweat sodden cigarette. He managed to get his passport back but he had to pay a few bribes and sign a form acknowledging that he owed the local taxes. I assured him it would be okay because I had a plan.

I made arrangements with a Sergeant I knew at Da Nang Airport who handled the manifest regarding those being transported on the C-130's going to Cubi Point, Philippines. He had strict instructions that all civilians, without special orders, must go through Saigon under the new immigration procedures. I was exempt from the instructions but Naugle wasn't. I gave the Sergeant a bottle of whisky and as a special favor; he put Naugle on the manifest. After arrival at Cubi Point, he could make his way to Manila and arrange a commercial flight back to Phoenix. He was glad to pay the one-way fare back to the US and I was pretty sure that Garrett would reimburse him anyway once he got back to Phoenix.

The hardest part was organizing to smuggle him out of Nam but I was determined to save his skin. Naugle was all smiles when I told him the plan. I went with him to make sure he got on the flight back to the world. He couldn't thank me enough, but was still quite nervous about what would happen when he arrived in Cubi. It all turned out well. No one even questioned him at the other end as to what he was doing on the flight and I don't think they cared.

****

June came and I was on the down hill side of my one year assignment. The heat coupled with the humidity was stifling. Along with the unbearable weather, Marble Mountain Air Base had to contend with something we hadn't counted on; the battleship USS New Jersey from the 7th Fleet anchored at Point Debbie off Marble Mountain. It was used to provide heavy bombardment that would offer support to troops fighting against inland and coastal targets. The underground entrenchments used by Charlie on our western perimeter were like rabbit warrens. There seemed to be more and more activity on our doorstep. Charlie would try again and again to over-run our western perimeter. They were reported to be "dug-in" and some drastic action had to be taken.

The New Jersey battleship was to be the answer. It was outfitted with 50, 16-inch guns. Bombarding would go on for days and sometimes through the nights, to defend our perimeter. It was nerve and teeth rattling, as the shells in most cases were going directly over our base to get to their targets. When I was on the flight line during the day the hangars and metal building would rumble dramatically each time the guns were fired. In the hooches, the corrugated metal would transmit each passing shot like a hi-fi speaker. The only thing worse would to be on the delivery or receiving end of the 16 inch round. For us it was just another burden to cope with; the noise along with the concern that one of the rounds of the Jersey might land short of their target, and into our laps.

Chapter 15
Visiting My Past and Seeing the Future

Up until this time, I had been sending a tape back to Doris and the kids almost every night that I was at MMAB but it was not possible to make or send tapes while up north. To carry the tape recorder around was not feasible, and the battery life was short. You couldn't count on base electricity as we had black outs frequently and often the electricity we had was not the correct voltage. Marble base had a large power requirement and the system could not keep up with the demand. I discovered that if I made a tape in the evening, I would sound like Donald Duck when it was replayed with the appropriate voltage. So if the lights in the hooch were dim or flickering, I would delay talking into the tape until they were bright and steady again.

It was good to get tapes from Doris, but I got less and less input from my kids. In all my tapes I would talk directly to each of them and ask them questions, sadly I wouldn't get any replies. It was also frustrating because Doris seldom spoke about anything other than superficial news. I was interested in what was going on in the world and about public opinion regarding the war. Doris didn't seem to care about anything much except me coming back to her.

By the end of her tapes I felt guilty because listening to her go on about how much she and our children wanted me home, I concluded that she was a very dull and uninteresting person. The only positive thing she spoke of was her accounting course, because it sounded like she was really enjoying it. That gave me some hope that she would branch out in her thinking and start to grow. With the positive news about her progress in the accounting course, I was beginning to think that I really needed to get my act together and think of the children and not myself. On the other hand, I wasn't at all sure that I was going to make it back to ever see any of them again.

When it came to Doris, my thoughts and feelings about my relationship with her were in a jumble. I had been the one to make her a child bride; and that made me feel even more responsible for her. Nine months after our marriage, she had our first child, Donna. Since Doris had left school to get married, I felt I needed to her encourage her while she furthered her education. However, I always noticed the look on her face of disappointment as I coaxed her each evening to work on her homework assignments. She had no confidence in herself but was extremely happy when she passed her exams and received her high school diploma.

I couldn't forget the separations, tough times, and major financial problems we had endured over the last ten years. And yet, she had stuck by me particularly when I was I was injured in the construction site accident. While in the body cast for three months and back brace for nine months, I was so debilitated that I was unable to bend over even to put my socks or shoes on.

Doris willingly did those things for me. I was disabled for over two years and our parents didn't have the means to assist us financially. We lived in one half of a converted barn during this period, almost hand to mouth. The winters were bitterly cold and it was hard to heat our living area because the walls and ceiling were not well insulated. I don't ever remember her complaining about the cold, or not having anything.

With the battle ship New Jersey still providing heavy bombardment over our heads each day it provided a good reason to arrange some R&R as soon as possible. I decided to spring for an airline ticket for Doris to meet me in Hong Kong in July. From Hong Kong, we could go together to Bangkok for a five-day visit before my return to Nam. The cheapest fare Doris could obtain was an "around the world" flight for US$1200. When she left Bangkok, she would have stops in Beirut, Rome, London, and New York before heading back to Pittsburgh. I hoped that this might spark some interest from her about the world outside the U.S. I was anxious to have the marriage work. I was starting to think that whatever the sacrifice on my part, it was worth trying a little harder to save the marriage, if I made it back.

****

Summer arrived and the heat coupled with the high humidity made every day feel like an outdoor sauna. It brought back memories of the summer heat I experienced in Paris Island, South Carolina when I went to Marine boot camp. I just took every day, one at a time. Time was passing and by now everything seemed to be routine. I was really an old salt and I could easily spot the FNG's and dazzle them with bullshit by telling war stories!

Life was pretty damn good, except for The New Jersey. I wanted to get out from under the constant pounding of the 16-inch guns and could justify a trip to Clark Air Force Base, in the Philippines, for a week before meeting with Doris in Hong Kong. The Air Force had overhauled a couple of T76 Garrett engines for the first time and wanted me to be there for the first test cell runs. That was just the excuse I was looking for.

I took a C-130 from Da Nang Main to Clark Air Force Base. I spent about five days at Clark and couldn't believe how similar it was to a large city in Mid West USA. The attitude was "chickenshit"; like a stateside assignment. Uniforms had to be clean with starched creases and all brass polished. Shoes had to be spit shined and a formal inspection was held every morning. Directly outside the main gate of the base was Angeles City, another "GI" town. It had a lawless atmosphere like Olongapo but was larger is size. Nothing but bars and bar girls. This place was only for the single men. The GI's along with their families stayed on the base and never had to leave the gates if they didn't want to.

I went off base and stayed in Angeles City the last night before departing for Manila. In a couple of days I would be with Doris and knew I couldn't take any chances at this point in time sleeping with another woman. I had a couple of close calls in the past with the enticing young women I'd met but managed to keep it in my pants. But, I had to see Angeles City for myself.

I went into one of the many nightclubs and struck up a conversation with a girl sitting at the bar. She was simply beautiful with natural white skin and what a body! She was well mannered and was very polite when she asked me if I would like to buy her a drink. She hadn't used a four-letter word in the past five minutes and didn't grab for my crotch. Her English grammar was better than mine and I found she had an advanced education. The more I spoke with her, the more intrigued I became. I was enjoying her so much and wanted to talk with her all night.

I was fully aware by now that the way the girls make the most money was to get "bought from the bar" to be taken home for the night. Any of the girls could be bought for anywhere from US$2 to $15. Fifteen dollars was more than most Philippine workers made in one month. She had a university degree in economics, but in the Philippines, this was the way she could make a large sum of money very quickly and she planned to be rich by investing her earnings in property.

I paid the $15 to the bar tender and she led me to a good restaurant. After dinner, she wanted to go back to my room. I couldn't resist on one hand but knew in my heart that I couldn't go through with making love with her. I was in one hell of a dilemma but by the time we entered my hotel room I had made it clear that I was going to meet Doris in two days. I was not going to do anything other than have some friendly conversation and I was going to get some sleep. It was one of the hardest things I had ever done. After a couple more hours we both became tired, cuddled up in bed and fell asleep in each other's arms.

Before she left my room the following morning she said: "You are the most kind man I have ever met"! "When you come back the next time I will go out with you for no charge and you can stay with me and the girls." I asked, "Where do you live?" "I live with the other girls"! Confused I asked, "What do you mean the other girls?" She smiled and said: "Another 20 girls that work at the bars." "They would love to meet such a nice man like you, but they might try to seduce you as a challenge!" My mind boggled!   Is that what heaven would be like, I asked myself. She handed me her personal card with her telephone contact. I quickly took it, gave her a good-bye kiss, and then closed the door. Was I mad? I wanted her more than anything else but I didn't want to think about it anymore.

My hormones would not settle down till I was almost in Manila in the comfort of the air-conditioned military bus that afternoon. I had just one night in Manila before catching the morning flight to Hong Kong. After I checked into the Carlton Hotel in Manila, I went out walking the streets and doing some window-shopping to kill some time before dinner.

As I walked from shop to shop window, a slender, young and good-looking woman running down the sidewalk in my direction took my attention because she seemed to be yelling at me. As she got closer she said: "I know you, I know you!" My first thought was, "another prostitute!" I just smiled and said to her, "I don't think so." She insisted, " I saw you in Hong Kong over Christmas." "You stayed at the Chung King Mansions and I would see you almost every day at the elevator going up to the rooms."

I was blown away, but had to concede that she must have seen me and I was impressed that she would remember. She said: I saw you looking into my shop window and I recognized you"! I walked with her back to her tourist shop to have a friendly conversation. She went on to tell me that she was in Hong Kong during the same week as I, on business. She went to Hong Kong twice a year to buy for her shop. It was hard for me to imagine that it was over 6 months since she saw me and we had never spoken. Yet, she spotted me in a crowd in a different country. It was good to talk to a local that wasn't a prostitute. She was a no nonsense, single, smart woman and had a good sense of humor, not to mention her well developed body filling her colorful silk blouse and skirt.

After spending an hour or so in her shop talking, she asked me to have dinner that evening at her home. I hesitated with my answer.... but decided against it. Frankly, it scared the hell out of me. It was too much of a test. I didn't know where it would lead. She was tempting and I didn't know if I could trust myself anymore. So I made my apologies and smartly got out of there before I changed my mind. I had an early dinner by myself and made it back to the hotel for a good night sleep in a clean quiet room.

On the 15th of July 1968 I arrived in Hong Kong on the flight from Manila. It was much hotter now than the last time I was here. But it was still much cooler than Vietnam or The Philippines.

I checked into the Chung King Mansions and went back to the airport later that afternoon to meet Doris. I had mixed emotions as I waited for her to walk though the arrival door. But all my negativity seemed to disappear as soon as I saw her. It was really good to see her. She was tired from the long flight but was over the moon to be with me after all those months of separation. It seemed like she had matured and I was really happy to see that. Asia was all new to her. The sights, sounds, smell and tastes were refreshing and I was happy to help her experience it for the first time.

We shopped and had custom tailored clothes and shoes made for her. We took day trips up to the New Territories and all our problems seemed to melt away. I had never seen her so interested or adventurous. I might have stretched the envelope since I last saw her, but I was glad I hadn't fallen into the arms of all the tempting women because I had no guilt to contend with.

Eleven days passed quickly and we were on the flight to Bangkok. We visited all the tourist spots we had time for. President Richard Nixon happened to be visiting Bangkok while we were there and we managed to see him getting out of his car with his entourage to attend a government meeting. The security was beyond belief. I had never seen so many snipers on buildings and helicopters flying overhead.

The next five days seemed to fly by. On one hand, I was sorry to see Doris going home to face the inevitable separation for at least another four months. But on the other hand, I was looking forward to going back to Vietnam. I had learned to enjoy my freedom.

I learned a lot during the time I spent with Doris on R&R. Since I had been in Vietnam I had changed in my way of thinking and we had grown even further apart in many ways. I really enjoyed her company while we were in such an unusual situation outside the United States because we could compare and talk about the different standard of living, foods and attitudes of the places we visited, but I wasn't at all sure I could handle living full time with her again.

In the end I came to the conclusion to commit myself to adjusting to family life again when I returned to the US and let bygones be bygones. Forgive and forget. There was too much hate, killing and animosity in the world. Somehow I had to think more of my children's future.

I saw Doris off on her return flight from Bangkok to Pittsburgh. She made the decision not to make any stopovers and head directly back to the States. She didn't have enough confidence to leave the airport terminals on any of the stops and have a look around on her own. I was a little disappointed but realized that being adventurous by herself was not part of her personality.

As soon as her flight departed I went to the military side of Bangkok Airport and hopped on a ride back to Da Nang on a DC-3. As we flew along the border of Thailand and Cambodia at low altitude, I could feel the adrenaline rush in anticipation of the adventure I knew would be returning to. As far as I could see on the horizon, there was nothing but jungle. I knew there had to be some villages along the way, but they went unseen, smothered by thick jungle. If we went down here, I calculated my chances of survival as almost zero. If the crash didn't kill you the elements or the hostile natives probably would.

By the time we crossed into Laos a short time later; I could almost feel my heart pounding as though it was my first date, but this wasn't my first date or first time. This time I knew exactly what to expect when I stepped off the DC-3. I couldn't wait to get back to Nam.

Chapter 16
In Country R&R

A couple of weeks went by since my R&R with Doris and it seemed like a year had passed. I received a telex that Ray Salverson had been assigned to a tour of duty in Saigon and he wanted me to meet him there. Within 24 hours, I made contact with Ray and arranged to meet at the Avco Lycoming office in Saigon and spend a long weekend.

Ray and I worked together as Engine Instructors for Avco Lycoming. We became good friends and our families had socialized. Ray was a very good looking, tall, and slender man a couple of years older than me. His hair was prematurely gray and he had a way with the women, so it seemed natural for him to be given the nickname "Silver Fox." In fact, women seemed to fall all over him. Soon after I left Lycoming I heard through the grapevine that Ray and his wife had divorced. He got itchy feet and transferred from the training department to Field Service.

As I landed at Saigon's Tan Son Nhat Airport I was overwhelmed by its size and the luxurious conveniences. The US Air Force made up the majority of the military force there and they had all the comforts of home. The base was like a small city of air conditioned quarters, banks, movie theaters, swimming pools, health clubs, rooms to listen to music or tape your own, and a huge PX that would rival any shopping center in the United States. I found myself wondering: Is this a war zone?

When I arrived at the Lycoming Office in the afternoon, it was much different to what I expected. I was overwhelmed by the grandeur of the place. The office was located on the ground floor of a French villa. High walls surrounded the villa with exposed broken glass bottles set into the top of the walls. Once past the iron-gate, I could see the beauty of the building. Marble steps led up to the main entrance. Marble pillars supported the upper level and to me, it looked like a small palace. The floors were of a black marble and the walls were all white marble. The high ceilings were graced with beautifully sparkling, crystal chandeliers.

When I walked into the office, it was like old home week. Ray was waiting for me as he said he would, looking more relaxed than ever. It was really good to see him and we hugged each other, like brothers reunited. He couldn't stop grinning. I knew just about everyone else in the office. Neil Mareska was the supervisor and had been in one of my classes as a student a couple of years before. Neil insisted that I take one of the guest rooms in the Lycoming Villa while I stayed in Saigon. He said that all the transient Lycoming Reps that came to Saigon on business from their "in country" assignment or those in transition in or out of the country used this villa. They had the luxury of a number of maids and housekeepers to do the cleaning and laundry. Then Neil said: "One house rule, no prostitutes are allowed in the house!" That was OK by me, because when I got back that evening, I just wanted some peace and quiet.

I looked at Ray and said: "This is a war zone?" "How can anyone have it this good?" Ray looked at me with one of his big smiles and said: "Isn't this the way life is meant to be?"

That night Ray and I went out with a couple other Reps to catch up on old times. I can't remember eating anything that night but I can remember the drinking. It was like being in a lawless city; men packed elbow to elbow in the bars. Go-Go Girls were dancing in cages hanging from the ceiling with bare breasts and scant G-strings, while other girls were dancing on a stage in the middle of the bar. There were as many as 50 to 100 girls working in each club and every girl was available as a prostitute. The music was loud and the drinks soon became monotonous as I fell into a drunken stupor.

Even in the middle of the night, Saigon was a beehive of activity. In the wee hours of the morning, I found myself riding in a rickshaw down a busy street; racing against other Lycoming Reps. The most popular mode of transportation was sitting in the front of these rickshaws with a "local" providing the man-power. We paid the drivers to race one another while we sat in the exposed seat, weaving in and out of the traffic trying to get ahead of each another. At road intersections I had to close my eyes, but each time we seemed to get through the maze of traffic without a scratch. The local drivers were hell bent to win the races because the winner would get a large tip from his passenger. The night only ended at daybreak, when it was time to get out of the sunlight and into a real bed in the villa.

Later in the morning after that first night, I woke up in a lather of sweat. My sheets were saturated with perspiration and I was hung over in the worst way imaginable. There was a floor fan in the distance blowing hot air in my direction. It was pretty ineffective. It was only mid morning and I had enough of the heat already. I was quick to learn that August is not a good month to be in Saigon. I got up, took a shower, and Ray and I went to get some fried rice for breakfast.

Ray suggested that we get away from the heat and the stagnant air, so we make a trip to Vung Tau that afternoon. He had been there before and knew his way around. We packed and made our way out to Tan Son Nhat Air Base through the heavy traffic and hitched a short ride on a C-130 to Vung Tau.

Vung Tau was an in country R&R destination for everyone and I mean "everyone!" It could be people from all the US forces, South or North Vietnamese or VC; yet, there was an "understanding" that Vung Tau would never be burdened with military aggression and friend or foe would not raise a weapon to one another. Everyone went there to get away from the war and, to my knowledge, there was never a person killed in the city of Vung Tau by military action.

The white, sandy beach town had a beautiful charm with French architecture easy recognizable on the buildings of the main street. The French had used Vung Tau as a resort town for decades before the "American" war.

We arrived before dark and checked into a hotel that Ray had stayed at before. The rooms were lovely with high ceiling fans and large window shutters that opened up to a view, across some lower buildings, to the South China Sea. The cool ocean breeze was blowing through the unobstructed windows. What a magical spot. Ray and I had connecting rooms with only a French louvered door to separate the two large rooms. I took a long shower after that hot, dirty trip and felt my batteries recharge. At dusk, Ray and I hit the street with enthusiasm.

Vung Tau reminded me of my short visit to Olongapo in the Philippines. Both sides of the main street were lined with bars. Round eye and local men in civilian clothes were crowding the sidewalks and moving in and out of the overcrowded bars. I wanted to start the evening with dinner as my breakfast had been ages ago. Ray wanted to have "one drink" before getting dinner. Agreeing to that drink was my first a mistake for the evening.

We went in, bought a drink at the bar and managed to find a table in a booth against the wall. The next thing I knew, five good-looking, young, local women were scooting into the booth with us. They started to talk to us with their broken accents. "Where you from?" "You buy me............" The few sentences they knew went on and on. "You handsome! I go home with you!" One drink turned into two then three and they kept coming. We bought the girls Saigon tea to add our support to the local economy and show them that our heart was in the right place! But I made up my mind that I would be going back to my bed at the end of the night by myself. I was tired and still hung over from the heavy drinking and antics of the night before.

A young Vietnamese boy, with a beautifully colored parrot in a cage, was going from table to table, trying desperately to sell it. The bird was amazing, and I hadn't ever seen a live parrot up close in my life. I wanted it, but knew I would have a difficult time getting it back to Da Nang. I also had no way to look after it when I was off on my trips up country, so I decided against it.

As the night went on things became more and more fuzzy. I was having a difficult time walking or thinking straight. I got back to the hotel without remembering how. I woke up the next morning not knowing where I was at first. My body and head were wracked with numbness, aches and pains. I was dehydrated and my body was in shock from alcohol and lack of food.

I was still trying to figure out where I was when I started to look around the room. Then I saw and heard something that brought it sharply into focus. My eyes were drawn in the direction of this ear piercing squawking noise, and then I spotted the parrot! What the hell? How did that get here, I wondered? Then I felt something soft touching me on the back of my neck. I would have jumped from the bed if my mind could have made contact with my arms and legs. I quickly reached to my neck and grabbed a soft yet bony hand. I turned around to see an anorexic looking Vietnamese girl lying beside me in my bed. She had so much make up on her face, she looked like she had fallen, face first, into a sack of flour. I looked at her and almost yelling I asked: "What are you doing here?"

She just gave me a big smile and said: "Do you like me?"

I then realized just how ugly she really was! She looked like she had been in a hatchet fight. Her face was pockmarked and scared and her body looked sadly underfed. I was speechless and amazed. I could not reply to her question and I could not take my eyes from her. I was in shock to think I picked this girl up for the night.

Just then, the adjoining room doors opened and Ray stuck his head around the door. His first words were, "I see you bought a parrot!" I was still confused about the chain of events that occurred last night and angry with myself at the same time. I didn't even have any rubbers for protection. I couldn't remember anything! "Get dressed, if you can pull yourself away from your girlfriend and we'll all go to breakfast," Ray said. He seemed to be chuckling to himself.

"My girlfriend" hesitated to get dressed as I headed for a quick shower. She sat on the edge of the bed and asked, "When do we make love; you said later?"

It was music to my ears! Thank God! I realized I had probably been too drunk to do anything the night before. Trying not to show my overwhelming relief, I said: "Better get dressed, we don't have time now."

Ray had picked up a good-looking girl the night before and she was hanging all over him as we walked down the street to the nearest restaurant. The girl I was with was trying to hold onto my arm and I was trying to keep her off of me. Now in the bright sunlight, I could hardly look at her unfortunate body and yet I felt sorry for her for being so ugly. Ray kept looking at us with his big grin.

Once I got inside the restaurant it hit me. How much money did I have remaining from the night before and did "my girlfriend" steal it. I was confused at first when I found that I had almost the same amount I had arrived with the day before. I knew the prostitutes could not get out of the bars without being paid in advance. This only meant one thing. Ray bought the parrot and the girl for me!

"Ray, you rotten son of a bitch", I exclaimed.

Ray knew the "jig was up", but still asked innocently, "What are you talking about?" He denied everything, but then, that was Ray, an artful prankster. He had a talent for finding a small crack in a situation and making a crevasse. I was still ecstatic that I hadn't had sex with the girl and that all I ended up with was a terrible hangover and a parrot. No harm done except to Ray's pocketbook and my liver.

That Sunday afternoon I made my way back to the airport to catch a direct flight to Da Nang. I had my trusty parrot in hand. I was beginning to like him more and more. When I went to the Sergeant to get on the C-130 manifest, he took one look at the bird in the cage and said: "The bird stays! Animals are not allowed to fly on military aircraft."

I told him: "It's not an animal......it's a bird!"

The Sergeant gave me a funny look as if trying to figure out my comment, then retorted: "It doesn't matter, the bird stays!"

There were a couple local Vietnamese families within my sight over on the edge of the tarmac. I walked over to one family with a young boy who had been waving to me. I handed him the bird and said: "Do you want him?" He gave me a big smile and took him.

As I walked back to the Sergeant to get on the manifest, I started wondering if perhaps the young boy was the same one who tried to sell me the parrot the night before!

R & R in Saigon

Ray (The Silver Fox") and I shortly after my arrival in Saigon.

Chapter 17
Reaching The Apex

My weekend away with Ray was like a wild dream. I was still recovering from the effects of the alcohol on Monday morning when I arrived on the flight line at Marble. I wasn't happy to find the New Jersey Battle Ship was still hammering away. Everyone's nerves were on the edge and there was more fighting within the ranks. I could see a marked "I don't give a shit" attitude, especially amongst the enlisted men. There seemed to be more marijuana and hard drugs than normal getting through from the cabbage patch and hooch girls. Now the heavy sweet smell of marijuana could be detected in the air every night.

I was quickly made aware of the turbine oil incident. A couple of Marines were selling turbine, synthetic oil to locals working on base. It was being marketed as cooking oil. Apparently, a large number of Vietnamese had died from poisoning before it was traced back to the turbine oil. It was "base news" for one day then never heard of again. There was never a hint of it in the Stars and Stripes.

That week didn't start off very well. We sent off one of the young and upcoming pilots to his death that morning. This was his first day back from his R&R in Hawaii. He and his wife met there and had spent 15 days together. I didn't visit the crash scene but was told: "He just went straight into the ground after dropping a white phosphorus rocket to mark a bombing position for an F-4 to bomb." His AO was killed also. I didn't know him as well but I went to the chapel that night for their Memorial Service. It was a sobering affair, but as soon as we went back to our duties the following day all the trauma was forgotten.

I was confronted with more bad news from my hooch mates. Their wives were relaying the antiwar sentiment that was taking place on a more regular basis in the US and around the world. The US was getting tired of the war and starting to question the validity of it all. There was a bad feeling amongst the troops that "Tricky Dickie" did not really want to win the war. If Nixon did, he would unleash the US Military to take over North Vietnam. Men were dying by the hundreds each week, for what? So the pockets of a few could be lined with money? The economy was strong in the US but at the cost of how many lives?

In August the New Jerseys' guns finally stopped. I must admit the incoming rockets and mortar from Charlie weren't nearly as bad during those three months. But soon after the New Jersey pulled up anchor, the incoming started all over again.

By now we were finding the engines were low on power and had to be prematurely removed at no more than 100 hours. If the sand erosion or foreign object damage to the compressor wasn't the reason the turbine/hot section was burnt out. The pilots did not monitor the Exhaust Gas Temperatures (EGT) as they should and without this monitoring, the EGT limits were always exceeded. They were only interested in having enough torque/horsepower for take-off, so this indication was the one they paid the most attention to. The hot weather conditions in Vietnam greatly reduced the horsepower capability of an engine. Numerous Engine changes were made each day for low power because the EGT limits were exceeded at every take-off. It was a constant battle to keep up with the ongoing engine repairs in the CER shop.

On the flight line more and more mistakes were made. One afternoon I was standing on the outside of a right hand engine on an OV-10 that had reported taking ground fire. A munitions man was about to load a gatling gun that was attached to the belly of the OV. The rotary weapon was turned slightly by hand and without warning; one round went off striking the nose wheel landing gear. A private standing directly beside the nose wheel was struck in the upper leg with shrapnel. The private fell to the ground about eight feet from me, moaning in agony and holding onto his leg that was already bleeding prolifically. I rushed over to assist a Master Sergeant already applying direct pressure to his wound. Soon after, the private was loaded onto a stretcher and taken to the hospital.

About a week later another major incident occurred. I was in a revetment discussing an engine problem with a pilot who had just climbed from his OV. About three revetments down from our location a munitions man was loading rockets into the pod of another OV. A rocket accidentally fired off and propelled across the ramp and into an adjacent empty revetment where it exploded on impact. I felt the concussion from the blast and dove to the ground for cover. Fortunately, within the protection of our revetment the airborne shrapnel went above our heads, but struck the tail of the OV beside us. A rain of hot debris was falling all around us. The pilot and I were lucky enough to be under the wing of the OV and even more lucky that the debris didn't catch the aircraft on fire.

The 1st MAW had one very experienced OV10 pilot who stood out above the rest. His hair was bright red and he was in his late twenties. He was given the nickname, Captain Red ("Baron"). I would see him go off every day when I was on the line at Marble and would have a chat to him on his return after engine shutdown.

One day it was business as usual at Marble and Captain Red was taking off to the south on the north/south runway. The OV was fully loaded with rockets for a sortie. It was a hot day and the TO weight was probably over gross. About halfway down the runway, Captain Red rotated, broke ground and started to climb. At about 50 feet, and while still over the last half of the runway, the left hand engine failed. The OV started to yaw heavily to the left as

Captain Red attempted to feather the failed engine to reduce the drag. But in the panic he shut down and feathered the right hand engine. With no engine power, the OV made a sharp turn to the left and started to roll over while heading directly for one of the maintenance hangars.

The copilot pulled the "D" ring as the OV was almost on its left side and Captain Red stayed with it all the way and inverted into the hangar. It exploded on impact. With all the noise around the flight line and in the revetment areas, I didn't see or hear anything until I heard the explosion of the impact. I looked up to see the hangar roof come off in a ball of flames. The concussion was unbelievable and most everyone was running for cover initially thinking that Charlie had dropped a 122mm rocket on the hangar. There was chaos for the remainder of the day and I was assigned to help in the accident investigation.

The copilot had ejected clear of the cockpit; but in an angle that did not allow his parachute to blossom fully and he was killed on impact when he fell to the taxi ramp. The fire brigade was there in a matter of minutes.. Emergency vehicles carried the survivors away. I was informed later that there were a few men in the burning hangar, but mostly support equipment was lost. I wondered, how many were a "few men." It was a sad day for all, and I never did get the answer to my question. I know Capt. Red and his copilot were killed, but it was impossible to tell how many others died inside the gutted hangar.

I can't recall any mention of these accidents in the Stars and Stripes. Perhaps they were too minor. What remained of the engines was removed and I viewed the engines for the analysis. My investigation revealed that the left hand engine had failed, due to a "de-couple" from the gas producer to the reduction gearing. Without a gear load, the engine gas producer over sped to the point of destruction. A new engine design was required. There was a requirement for a direct drive fuel control system so the fuel control over speed fuel governor (OSG) could sense a gas producer over speed in the event of a de-couple. This was a major change in the gearbox and it would take more than a year to design and certify. Meanwhile the military had to continue to operate with this "soft spot" in the engines, by routinely carrying out premature gearbox inspections.

The official accident investigation team reported the incident to be "pilot error." If only Capt. Red had not shut down and feathered the right hand engine, he might have been able to maintain control of the OV or fly it over the South China Sea to bail out safely. The South China Sea beach line was only another 200 to 300 yards from the crash site however, I wasn't too sure he could have made the distance because I believed the aircraft was well over gross weight and would probably have run out of rudder control with just a single engine.

Chapter 18
Fuck it I'm Short

On one of my usual trips up to Quang Tri from Marble, we got side tracked for some unknown reason and landed the CH-46 at Lao Bao. It was right on the border of Laos and fewer than fifteen miles south of the DMZ. It was one of the points of entry into South Vietnam from the Ho Chi Min Trail. There had been a big "mop up" going on over the last couple of days and the Marines were being airlifted out again. This was an ordinary occurrence. The US would go in, secure an area with, sometimes, heavy loss of life, and then leave again. We never lost a battle but would walk away from what had been gained, leaving the area for the enemy to reestablish. A few weeks later the same thing would happen all over again.

After landing the CH-46, the mud covered grunts started boarding through the rear ramp with a cache of arms that they threw on the deck of the helicopter. A stack of AK-47's, M-16's, 38 and 45 caliber weapons were at my feet. One injured Marine was loaded. Even though assisted by a comrade, he was walking of his own free will. I couldn't see anything but mud and blood on his uniform. It would have been impossible to tell where he was hit except for the red stained white gauze around his forearm. Most of the heavy casualties had been medivaced out a little earlier.

The arm signals from the Flight Crew Chief indicated that there was no more room in the chopper. By now, I felt like a sardine in a can and thought we might be overloaded. Fortunately I was sitting in one of the sling seats close to a window. The ear penetrating, whine of the engines indicated the Sea Stallion was about to lift off and as the pilot pulled collective we almost blew the remaining grunts off their feet. We struggled to break free from ground effect, but with the nose down and a little air speed we continued our climb.

We headed almost due east and landed in Quang Tri. After landing the pilot shut the engines down. It was finally quiet except for the grunts shouting orders as they were getting clear of the chopper. As the weapons were being unloaded, I ask the Gunny Sergeant, "Where did all the weapons come from?"

He looked at me with half a smile and said: "We picked them up off the dead Gooks as war souvenirs!"

"Why are there so many US weapons", I asked?

"Over a period of time, the Gooks took them from our dead, and sometimes the same weapon gets passed back and forth a couple of times."

Wishing I had a couple of them, I asked, "What are you going to do, keep them all?"

"We'll sell most of them for a beer party!"

I looked over some of the guns still at my feet and asked, "How much do you want for them?"

His quick reply was, "Ahh, $5 each, take your pick!" It didn't take me long to pick out three M16's two AK47's and one 45 caliber pistol. One of the AK's had shrapnel damage to the stock and receiver. I thought it would make a fantastic war souvenir and conversation piece.

Reaching into my pocket I said: "How about $20 for these six; since this AK is inoperable from shrapnel"! He looked at me, hesitated, then smiled and took the $20 from my hand. I must have looked like a gunrunner as I walked down the flight ramp and through sniper alley making my way to the "Tiltin Hiltin." That afternoon I cleaned the weapons, gathered up some ammo and went out to the river perimeter for a shoot. Don and I threw cans or what ever would float into the water and blew the hell out of them. Every weapon worked well; but I didn't trust the damaged AK enough to do a test fire with it. I was thrilled with my purchase. I gave one of the M16's to Don and a couple days later carted my cache back to Marble.

I planned to keep the two AK's for myself along with one of the M16's and the 45cal pistol. I decided I would give the other M16 to Rick Colerick. But somehow, I had to get them back to the US. At the end of their tour in Vietnam, many of the Marines had their "war souvenirs" shipped with their personal items back to their base camp in the US without customs inspection. After all, it was a time of war and a small infringement like shipping weapons didn't raise an eyebrow. I had been able to ship engine parts back to Phoenix for special inspection or failure analysis without customs inspection, so I hoped that this technique was going to be my ticket to getting them home.

The Sergeant in charge of shipping was very accommodating for the cost of a bottle. I wrapped each gun separately in a bubble wrap then wrapped all of them together in a strong, silver fiber, oilcloth. From the outside it could have easily been anything other than guns. Then all over the outside I wrote, "PERSONAL PROPERTY of Richard Ingelido", "DO NOT OPEN", and "Contact Rick Colerick Field Engineering Dept: 77-3S" (with his telephone extension).

I sent Rick a letter well in advance of the shipping, telling him to be on the look out for this particular shipment marked for his attention and let him know I had a surprise in it for him!

Jerry was getting out of hand. He was drinking heavily every night, sleeping in, and hardly ever sober during the day; consequently I didn't see him much on the flight line. The drinking sessions, with his buddies partying in his partitioned room, continued for most of the night.

Eventually one night came the straw that broke the camel's back. Jerry returned to the hooch well past midnight. Everyone had settled down and was sleeping soundly. He turned the lights on then started yelling, while staggering back and forth from the front entrance to the back. I sat up in bed and yelled at him, "Jerry, shut the fuck up and go to bed!" Then I noticed that he had something in his hand just above his head. It was a grenade! Trying to be calm I asked, "What are you trying to do Jerry?"

Jerry slurred out a short sentence: "Blow this fucking place all to hell!" We were all out of bed by now. Jerry declared while weaving around the middle of the floor: "Don't try to stop me, the pin is pulled!" Now everyone was wide-awake and trying to talk some sense into him.

"Calm down, do you want to kill all your friends? Where's the pin, Jerry? Let's put the pin in the grenade and we'll all go to bed." He started laughing and suddenly seemed to be sobbing.

"I hate this fucking place", he said, then slowly raised the grenade higher in the air. Everyone backed off from him in fear and confusion. Suddenly he walked to the back porch, opened the screen door and pitched the grenade out onto the sand. Everyone except for Jerry ran for cover and in a couple of seconds there was a loud bang. The grenade was either a dud or a training grenade and didn't explode properly. Jerry was now laughing his ass off, acting like it was a big joke. Every one of us was angry enough to tear a piece from him, until we saw the look in his eyes. He was scared, drunk and mentally screwed up all at the same time. We thought it best to just put him to bed.

One of the base MPs arrived after all the commotion. They let Jerry stay in the hooch and sleep it off that night but the next day they came by to take him to see the Commanding Officer. A short while later a replacement arrived and Jerry was on his way back home to Texas. He was going to need some help when he got there. I heard through the grapevine that he got the axe when he returned to Bell. None of us ever heard exactly what happened to Jerry in the long term.

Several months after Doris' visit, I woke up one morning and thought to myself, I'm getting short -- so short that I could walk under a table and not hit my head. My year was just about up and I hadn't seen any orders for my transfer stateside. I left Camp Pendleton on November 2, and it was only a couple of weeks until that date would roll around again. I went to the CO at Da Nang Main and asked what was going on.

The desk-sergeant sent a telex back to Washington DC inquiring into my transfer. The following day I was called back to the office to find that I was to stay on for one additional month beyond my year. I would not be replaced; in fact, the Marines were going to be pulled out of Dong Ha, Quang Tri and Phu Bai by November 1 of 1969. The US military force was pulling out in a "systematic withdrawal" and the 1st MAW would be one of the first to go. It would be handed over to the RVNs. The plan was for me to stay until all the OVs were out of the northern sector. Some of them would be moved to Okinawa, some to the Philippines and the remainder absorbed at Marble. All I knew was the cold weather was returning along with more frequent rainstorms and I didn't want to spend another winter here.

Things started changing rapidly. Don Schmitt, Michael Bell and Jewel Langford got their orders and were shipped back. On the day they returned to Phoenix they were given their walking papers. Garrett Corporation seemed to have no place for the very Reps that had risked their lives to take care of the T76 engines. No contract meant no job. The economy in the aircraft industry was turning sour. Due to the winding back, the US government wasn't spending and production was coming to a grinding halt. Gary McIntire had been assigned to the Air Force at Danang Main to replace Don Naugle who had previously returned to the U.S. Gary would stay on with that assignment, but from now on, it was clear that any Rep that lost his contract in Vietnam would have no assignment on return to the U.S. Nobody wanted to return to the Real World to face that consequence.

People were coming and going, but mostly going, and the mood of the new men was no longer gung ho or "let's get the job done." No one wanted to be here. Coming from the States where they had been subject to the negativity of the protesters made being stationed here a lot harder. All the older grunts I had made close friends with went home in one way or the other. As soon as the last Marine was moved from the northern bases, the Cong and NVA moved in to take up the positions. The plan was for U.S. troops to pull back to Hi Van Pass and hold everything south of Da Nang. The sad thing was that the RVN could not hold the ground. At times they were overrun and at others they just deserted. Everyone was pissed at the hopeless situation. We remembered all the lives that had been lost to hold land that we were now just giving to the enemy. We never lost a battle, but we were losing the war.

I was starting to wonder if I was ever going to get out of there when, at last, my orders came through about the 10th of November. I was to depart Da Nang on the last day of November and report back to Pax River Naval Air Test Center. That was a relief, because the message to me was, the government planned to take care of me…for now.

The new contract was only for three-months, but it would give me time to get back and adjust to the real world. I could also look for a job that didn't require me to be away from my family again. The added bonus of this assignment was that Pax River was close enough to drive back to Connellsville each weekend to be with my family. I also realized that I would be home for Christmas to see my kids – that is if I managed to stay alive for about three more weeks.

I hadn't known fear for quite some time, but now I felt a hint of it creeping up on me. This must be Stage Three in the mental cycle and it wasn't a good feeling. In my time here I knew that it wasn't unusual for someone to be killed a couple of weeks before their tour of duty was complete. The expression

I heard over and over from short timers was, "Fuck it, I'm short!" I know now, that the phrase meant that we were more afraid than normal and hyper-vigilant. Don't take any unnecessary chances, I kept telling myself; I just might make it after all.

I couldn't help but think about the rocket attack that occurred just a few days before I knew my "going home" date. At about 10:00PM, a rocket shot directly over the NCO Club and landed on the beach. It landed in the soft sand less than 50 yards from the Club without causing damage or injury. Over 100 men in the club ran for the safety of the outside bunkers that night. While the frantic men were running across the sand en route to the bunkers, another rocket landed in the middle of the Marines who were out in the open. The explosion killed at least twelve men and countless were injured. Fortunately the sand absorbed much of the impact otherwise the casualties would have been much higher. It was like playing Russian roulette and the longer you played the worse your chances of survival were. I was ready to stop playing.

A few days later a Corporal came by the hooch to tell me that the Base Commander wanted to see me. I wasn't alarmed, as I had met him in the past. When I walked into his office he had a long look on his face. Then he said: "Here's a letter from the Tobacco and Firearms Division of the FBI," and handed me an envelope with a government seal on the outside. Sign here that you received this. I don't know what it's all about, but it looks pretty official and I never hear from those guys unless there is major trouble."

I signed the piece of paper and quickly opened the envelope to find a notice requesting my presence in Washington DC. I went on to read, the words - You are under investigation for smuggling contraband.   Holy shit! It was like getting hit with lightening! My orders had already been approved for transfer back to Pax River. The Tobacco and Firearms Division must have known this and instructed me to report to their main office in Washington DC, since it was only a short drive north of Pax River. I had been looking forward to going back to the US, but now I was concerned. I might be going from Vietnam straight into a US jail! I preferred Vietnam on those terms. My imagination was running wild. How could this happen to me? Thousands of men had shipped guns back and hadn't been caught. Why me? How come my "Personal Items" package got checked? I was full of questions, with no one to ask and no answers.

I was afraid that I would need the money I saved while here to pay attorneys and court costs. I could be broke and in jail. What would my kids think of me if I went to jail? How would I provide for them? A month was too long to wait for the interrogation and the suspense was unbearable. I walked out of the Base Commanders' Office with my tail between my legs.

I made one more trip to the Navy PX along Highway One going north to Da Nang. Except for the Air Force PX at Da Nang Main, it was the biggest store and had the best selection of duty free items. I needed to buy a suitcase, some new civilian shoes and a couple pair of pants before I made my trip back to the US. I was gearing down and had planned on leaving everything behind except for my new suitcase and civvies. I sold my position in the hooch and I had a buyer for the trusty Honda from a ROK Marine with a high kill rate and a lot of money in his pocket. He would get the motorcycle the day before I left Marble for the US. It would give me money in my pocket before I shipped out, since all my pay was going back to Doris. She had to pay the bills and I hoped she was putting a chunk into savings. I had been living on my daily allowance for the last year.

I rode the Honda to the front gate of the PX that was now guarded by ROK Marines. There was a secure area at the gate, and I parked the Honda in an area surrounded by cyclone fence and barbed wire. I walked into the PX and did my shopping. An hour later I came out to find the Honda was missing! I asked the ROK Marine guard, "Where's my Honda?" He looked at me with a blank look on his face and shrugged his shoulders.

I was really pissed off! "You were supposed to be watching it", I yelled at him. He just gave me a dirty look and I knew it was a waste of time trying to pursue it. I guessed that if he didn't steal it one of his buddies had. I caught the next cargo truck back to Marble and now had another worry. I wouldn't have near the amount of cash in my pocket that I thought I would. When I told the ROK Marine of the misfortune, he didn't seem to care much about the loss. He didn't even ask me any questions or tell me, "too bad." I got a sinking feeling that he might have been instrumental in the missing Honda. He knew about my plans for a final trip to the Navy PX. I couldn't prove anything, but was starting to be even more skeptical of my fellow man. I was almost positive that he had my Honda stashed away until after my departure.

In my last couple of days I could see more signs of the RVN, in desperation, trying to take over a lost cause. Almost daily they would fly over Marble Air Base in their S58 Sikorsky helicopters. Hanging from the chopper on a rope would be a VC they were interrogating. As it flew over the Marble Mountains, barely missing the peaks, the suspended man was pulled inside and information requested. If the VC didn't tell them what they wanted, he was lowered out again to make a couple more passes at the hills. In the end, if the RVN weren't satisfied, the man would "accidentally" fall out of the chopper from about 500 feet and plummet to his death!

Chapter 19
Back to the Strange World

Finally, the end of November arrived along with my departure day. I was still uneasy about climbing aboard the MAC-V flight heading back to the real world. I was mentally exhausted from the weeks of uncertainty. I was in a dilemma at times whether to head to another country or to take a chance with Tobacco and Firearms and end up in jail. I didn't want to face up to the gun issue that was hanging over my head. After scrutinizing all my options, I came to the conclusion that the only way I would ever be "free" again would be to face up to my screw up.

After a short stop over in Guam, we landed at the Naval Base in San Francisco. From there I had a debriefing, caught a cab to the San Francisco Airport and purchased the first seat possible on a flight back to Phoenix. I called Doris from San Francisco to let her know that I was back in the US, and in one piece. I hadn't told her about the gun smuggling incident yet and wasn't about to tell her until I saw her face to face. There was no reason for both of us to worry about it. I also knew that Doris would be on the phone with her mother right away trying to get her advice. I didn't want to listen to what my mother-in-law had to say!

When I arrived in Phoenix, I couldn't wait to get checked into a hotel and phone Rick Colerick. I needed to find out what he knew and what he told the authorities. Up to this time I had been very close with Rick and hoped that this incident did not destroy that relationship. I knew I had stretched the limits and felt he was, at the very least, disappointed with my foolish action.

Rick's voice was very concerned and to the point. "I didn't know what was going on. Apparently, when your personal items arrived in our shipping department, one of the men opened the sealed package instead of contacting me as per the instructions on the package. When they saw the contents, they told their supervisor who in turn called the FBI."

"Why the hell did they open it?" I asked in amazement.

Rick didn't answer this but went on to say, "The first thing I knew about it was when the FBI came to my office and started asking me questions regarding the package of smuggled guns. I couldn't tell them anything since I really didn't know what was in the package. The senior Garrett management wants to have you replaced, but I've managed to fend them off for now. Let's see what happens at your interrogation in DC." Then he kindly asked if I wanted to tell him what happened at my end.

I explained all the details about how I obtained the guns and the method of shipment. "One had your name on it", I said.

Rick's quick reply was, "What? Did it?"

I assured him that he could relax because his name had only been on the gun "in my head". Rick didn't know that one of the guns was to be his present. Then he said in a very considerate way, "By the way, welcome back and how the hell are you?" I knew then that Rick was not upset with me and we were still friends. "You'll get through this", he said in a reassuring tone. I felt much better after I hung up the phone. My worst fear was the loss of respect from the people close to me.

I made contact with Pax River to find that my "Special Contract" had been reclassified and downgraded to a "Standard Military Contract." It only required the Tech Rep to have a Secret Clearance. I wasn't being replaced yet, but I knew Garrett would not have a difficult time covering the Pax River contract, since so many other military contracts were cancelled. I also knew that if I didn't come out clean from the meeting with the Tobacco & Firearms people, no one would be able to save me.

I stayed in Phoenix a couple more weeks before heading back to Connellsville to spend the Christmas holidays with my family. Everyone at Garrett gave me a big welcome back. They were stopping me in the halls wanting to talk with me. I had an uneasy feeling answering all the questions about what it was like in Vietnam and what a fucked up situation the U.S. was in. They acted like I was a hero; but I didn't feel like one. In fact I felt guilty about the attention. I didn't feel like I accomplished anything valiant or compassionate, in fact to the contrary. We were loosing the war and much worse I felt like we were doing more harm to the South Vietnamese people than good with the war dragging on. I was having a hard time adjusting when I heard the lies and deception that were being given to the public by the media and the government. All the turmoil going on in the U.S. made it more difficult for me to make any sense of my own purpose.

My first day back in Connellsville was a shock. Doris greeted me happily; but I wouldn't have expected anything else. However, my kids were all very distant and disinterested in me. There was a snowstorm and it was freezing cold outside. Even though my kids were inside, they just played by themselves. I couldn't get close to them. It appeared that reuniting with them was going to take longer than I thought.

Later, when Doris told me that Donna and Doug had been doing poorly at school; I went to visit their teachers. The thing that hit me the hardest was when the teacher said: "Donna talked about you every day. She missed you terribly and was angry with you for leaving her."

Doug's teacher said: "He just doesn't have the attention span and is not interested in anything." When I got back to our apartment, I found it difficult to get Donna to talk to me. In fact, she seemed to look at me like she didn't care about me at all. Trying to talk to Doug was not easy either. He looked at me, appeared to be listening, but it seemed my words were falling onto deaf ears.

His reactions to my questions were, "Yes, No, or I don't know!" I couldn't get him to open up to me, no matter how hard I tried but I felt relieved that he didn't appear to dislike me. This was only his first year at school and he had plenty of time to get it together, but I knew that he had to get off on the right foot. I didn't want to scold either of them. I knew that if I did that would probably drive them further away. All in all, there was a huge change in their attitude toward me. It will take time I told myself, but I'll make it up to all of them. I'll be a good father from here on, if I get past the gun smuggling obstacle.

I was soon to find that Doris didn't save near the money I had hoped. I was disappointed, but happy that at least she paid off the car and the other outstanding bills. I was thrilled that Doris had finished her accounting course with top honors and I felt like a monkey was off my back. I hoped that she would get a job and some outside interests. I was looking forward to not being smothered as I had been in the past.

I started to run into a few other problems on my first week back in Connellsville. Doris and I were invited to a Christmas party in the apartment complex where she and the kids were living. There were a number of educated people there. Some were teachers and one Democratic Council member. The word got around very quickly that I had just arrived back from Vietnam. It seemed as though everyone at the party was against the Vietnam War. It started slowly, but the more people drank the worse the insults toward me became. Doris didn't understand what was going on. Some of the abusers were putting Doris down, for not knowing about the war and for being married to me.

I tried not to get angry, but I really felt like smashing someone's face into a wall. I kept telling myself that they were trying to get me to act aggressively confirming that all men who went to Vietnam are aggressive psychopaths. Then someone said: "Anyone who goes to Vietnam is a baby killer!" That was enough for me to get the hell out of there before I totally lost control and ended up in jail for hurting someone. Overall it was a rotten Christmas and I was unsettled even more than ever. I felt more pressure than I had ever experienced in my life. I wanted to run away, but knew I couldn't. Some how I had to get my feet back into "the real world."

Christmas was cold, with blowing snow, and by the end of my visit, things were still on the cool side with my kids. I made my way to Pax River after New Year and reported in with my orders. I had been there before I went to Vietnam and knew my way around. Most of the faces had changed, but the base and the attitude was still the same. Garrett was experimenting with an engine Single Red Line System (SRL) and was about to put it on a Marine OV-10 for test and acceptance flights. This was an interesting program, but for now, my mind was still occupied with my pending visit to Washington DC.

When the day came to drive to Washington, I felt myself shaking uncontrollably inside. I could hardly hold my foot steady on the accelerator pedal. It felt as if someone else was driving my body and I was just an innocent bystander observing from the sidelines. By not being in touch with reality was probably my self defense mechanism kicking in.

I made up my mind that I was going to be perfectly honest in my responses to their questions. The only thing I would not do would be to give the names of anyone who might have "assisted" me. As far as I was concerned, no one, other than me knew that I was shipping anything other than engine parts. I was asked to send in a written statement and have it notarized just after I returned to Phoenix. I did this and before I went to DC I reread the copy over and over again to make sure I was totally accurate. The agents would have had time to study my statement then ask me questions to clear up any gray areas. I didn't want to complicate things further with lies.

Once I found the Tobacco and Firearms Division and reported to the desk, I was taken to a dimly lit room with bare walls. When the two agents walked in, they formally introduced themselves and told me of the charges I was facing. It caught me off guard and I was shocked when they said: "We have you on about ten different charges. The main ones are smuggling contraband, shipping illegal (automatic) weapons, shipment of arms across state borders, misuse of military shipping and unlawful use of the U.S. Postal System. I felt weak in the knees and half expected handcuffs! I was thinking that I should have taken the run away option.

I was asked to sit in the middle of the long side of a rectangular table in the center of the room. I found it difficult to see the faces of the two agents. A single light was hanging above the table but was so low it was glaring in my eyes when I sat down. They sat on the other side of the table, at right angles or close to each end. If one asked a question I had to turn my head 90 degrees from one agent to look at and answer the other agent's question. In this way one could ask me a question and the other could observe my expressions. They kept asking questions, back and forth, back and forth. Usually, I was not allowed to finish my reply before the other agent cut in with another question. They kept covering the same things over and over but asked in different ways until my brain cells felt dead.

"Whom did you buy them from? Did you know the guns were operational? Did you fire the guns? How many times? What gun did you fire the most? How many rounds did you fire in your favorite weapon? What were you going to do with them? Where did you get the ammo to fire the AK47s? Surely you know who gave you the ammo! How many rounds did they give you? Where did they get the ammo? Where did you fire them? Who was with you? Who gave you the oilpaper to wrap the guns for shipment? Who else saw you wrap the guns for shipment? Who were you going to sell them to? Why did you want so many guns?" I tried to tell them that the whole business was all my own doing. I agreed that there were other people who might have known about them, but they weren't involved in any way. I kept saying these things in different ways.

After four hours or so, the agents started to lighten up and asked me general questions about the war and how it was going. They wanted to hear more about the part I played. In the end, they told me they had test fired all my guns on their firing range and all were found to be operational. I told them of my particular interest in the AKs as one was Russian made and one was Chinese. We talked about the guns for a while and they told me they enjoyed shooting them. Then one of the agents said: "We are having a big problem with smuggled guns going to the Black Power Movement. We wanted to make sure you weren't a part of that in any way."

"What would you say to a license fee for the four automatic weapons?" one finally said.

I stared blankly at him, felt confused and asked what he was talking about. The other agent said: "We can't see where you meant any harm, so we are giving you a way out. If you pay $800 for the gun license, we will let you go without formal charges and the license fee won't be seen as a fine against you."

I could have jumped for joy, but couldn't help but ask, "Do I get to keep the guns then?"

The agents looked at me in amazement and with a smile said: "No, we keep them, you just pay."

It still sounded like a hell of a good deal to me, so I agreed to the conditions, thanked them both and there were smiles all around. I was free after months of worry! The new year of 1970 had just begun and I felt a whole new world had opened up for me. In a few more weeks I would be 30 years old and I needed to get my life together. I still had many issues to resolve, but at least I was free to do so.

Epilogue

After three months at Pax River, Maryland on the military assignment, I was hired into the commercial (civil) side of Garrett as a Field Engineering Representative on the Garrett TPE331 Turboprop Engine. I wasn't working for Rick Colerick anymore. After a month of training in Phoenix, I moved to Philadelphia to prepare for my families' arrival. In June of 1970 all five of us were back together again. Over the last two years, we had only spent three months, together as a family. There was a great deal of adjustment for all of us.

Trying to adjust to civilian life after Vietnam was daunting. Dealing with civilian customers was difficult, I felt like a fish out of water. If I talked about Vietnam outside the family I'd get a negative reaction – like I'd been to prison for murder. No one understood and I felt guilty and frustrated. I was still unsettled when six months later, on the Philadelphia assignment, I was laid off. Garrett called on a Thursday night to say Friday would be my last day! It was a cold and cruel way to lose a job, at a time when the job market was pitiful. The major military cutbacks to the war effort had affected the U.S. economy, which made it very difficult to find any type of employment.

During the two years after my lay off, Doris and I went through major problems, eventually leading to a separation. I was not able to cope with her or myself. She was unwilling to get a job to financially assist. We had moved from Philadelphia to Reading Pennsylvania in an attempt to find steady employment. I was in and out of five different jobs, drawing unemployment checks and living from hand to mouth. I started dating another woman to add to the problems. I was completely broke and at one time got to the point of sleeping in the back of a grounded DC3 during the middle of a bitter Reading winter. My relationship with the kids had also reached its coldest peak. I was in the depths of despair and almost gave up all hope of life ever being normal again. Then I was offered a position as Customer Liaison with Airwork Engine Overhaul Agency in Milville, Jersey. Doris and I patched things up one more time and we made the move as a family to New Jersey. I wasn't making much money and had to work long hours, but it was a steady job.

About two and a half years after my return from Vietnam, Rick called me one day out of the blue to ask if I wanted to come back to Garrett on the new TFE731 fan engine program. I would be assigned to the certification of the Gates Lear Jet 35/36 in Wichita, Kansas as a Factory Representative, Installation Engineer. This call was fantastic for both work and personal reasons. Would I? Of course I would! I was looking forward for another opportunity to get my life back together again.

Doris and I were back together for a short while, but again it didn't work. In Wichita, my daughter, Donna became pregnant when she was 14 years old and elected to have an abortion. She was always in trouble at school and ran away from home for days at a time. Counseling was unsuccessful and she acted like she hated the sight of me. I was totally frustrated with her and myself and didn't know what to do. Things were so bad that Donna would leave any room I walked into. I couldn't stand to be home any more. Doris blamed me for the problems, made me feel guilty and constantly pressured me to stay with her. I felt certain that her refusal to find employment enabled her to remain dependent. She was smothering me and the two years in Wichita were riddled with problems and more separations.

I felt depressed and became involved with Judy Lea during one separation. She was a secretary at Gates Lear, a 27-year-old divorcee with a great personality, very smart and totally independent. I found myself with feelings I had forgotten were possible. After a few months of dating and a lot of manipulation from Doris, I decided to end my relationship with Judy and return to the family. I was offered a company transfer to be the first Customer Service Engineer on the TFE731 engine in Phoenix. It would be a permanent position at the factory and a promotion. I saw this as another chance to start afresh.

We moved back to Phoenix in an effort to start our new life. By moving away we hoped Donna would lose contact with her undesirable friends and change her circumstances. Shortly after the move cracks turned to voids, I was drinking heavily, depressed and extremely unhappy, and my life was out of control. Within a year, I moved out for the last time and Doris agreed to a divorce. The divorce became final on April 3, 1975 and soon after, I phoned Judy in Wichita and proposed marriage. Doris detested Judy and wrongly blamed her for our marriage break up.

On the 4th of July 1975, Judy and I were married in Los Vegas. It turned out that the fireworks were indoors! We had a huge argument early in the evening over my gambling and Judy locked me out of our hotel room for the night. It wasn't a good way to start a marriage. There were many reasons why my second marriage was unstable from the very beginning. My depression and post war problems, together with the suffering and guilt I felt over the loss of my children combined with Judy's extreme jealousy of Doris and children, as well as her resentment of the burden of child support payments, which absorbed about 70% of my paycheck, were all too much.

Shortly after we married, I took a field engineering assignment with Falcon Jet in Teterboro, New Jersey. I thought that leaving Phoenix would help. It didn't, and Judy started drinking heavily from the pressures in our marriage and my frequent absence due to my work's grueling schedule.

To my dismay, I heard my good friend Rick Colerick had died of a heart attack, he was just 43, then about a year later Don Schmitt died from a heart attack also at about the same age. Don was screwed up from Vietnam, and he was alcohol dependent at the end. He left his wife for another woman, but she walked out on him during the first month for another man! Two of my closest and best friends were gone. I missed being able to pick up the telephone almost any time to talk about our troubles. It all came to such an abrupt end – it made it very hard to cope without their support.

In the middle of the night on February 23, 1976, Doris called me at home in Teterboro and muttered two devastating words: "Donna's dead!" There was a long silence between us before I could absorb the impact of these two words. This was the most unbelievable and heart-wrenching news a father could receive. She had died of substance abuse in the bedroom at a girlfriend's house. God, she was only 16 years of age and I felt devastated.

I boarded a flight to Phoenix the next morning, in a state of shock and denial, to make the funeral arrangements. During the flight my mind was in turmoil. With all the problems we'd had, I felt anguish and yet relief that she was dead. Immediately I felt guilt like never before; what kind of warped mind did I have? I felt absolutely gutted. Later that day, I tried to talk to Doug and Denise about Donna's death. They were unable to show any emotion or accept her death. The three of us just stood outside their house looking at footprints left by Donna the day before, in the sand of the desert landscape. It was like she was still with us. The next evening I watched the casket being loaded into the cargo hold of the aircraft and finally it all started to sink in. It was a sad flight back to Pittsburgh I sat in the cabin and quietly cried. Her service and final resting place were just outside of Scottdale, Pennsylvania.

The torture of this experience was made worse by petty family jealousy. Doris hated Judy so much that she didn't want her to attend Donna's funeral. I didn't want a scene at the funeral home so I asked Judy to honor the request. To make matters worse, my mother entered the fray; she believed that Judy should be at my side. Judy was furious with my decision and we separated not long afterwards. Our divorce was final on Jan 24, 1977 but we continued to date and support one another.

I still had a great love for Judy and I know she felt the same way about me. I wanted to help her with her drinking problem and somehow put some sanity back my life. Judy and I both decided to stop drinking so heavily and things improved. She wouldn't just live with me, so we decided to remarry a second time. Judy wanted total commitment. My third marriage on 4 July 1977 turned out to be a bigger mistake than the second. Judy started drinking more than ever and was extremely aggressive toward me, and life in general.

In the meantime Garrett transferred me to Long Beach, California. After another one of my demanding business trips, I came home to find my clothes in a stack on the garage floor and the locks on the doors of the house all changed. It was less than a year since our marriage and we were back to the divorce lawyers again. This time the divorce took place in California and Judy took what little I owned and burned what she didn't want. I was in my late thirties and flat broke again, but at least I had solid employment.

I was offered and accepted an overseas assignment in Singapore for three years. It came at just the right time, and I hoped, once again, to build up my cash reserves. There were no TFE731 fan powered aircraft so it would be back on the TPE331 turboprop engine again. I had an assignment to cover all Garrett customers from Nepal to Papua New Guinea. The area is equal to twice the distance across the U.S. My home office was in Singapore at the Garrett engine overhaul agency, but to cover my area I traveled over 90% of the time. I spent months at a time traveling from country to country, living in hotels and in many poor living conditions.

It was a lonely life, as many of my customers didn't speak much English and I had very little to entertain myself in the evenings. Hotel living was monotonous after all the sights were seen and there was nothing but boredom to contend with. Nothing happens very fast in Asia. A task that would normally take one day to do in the U.S. took two weeks to a month in most cases.

In a small isolated village on the island of Java in Indonesia I came down with malaria. If it not for the kind heart of the cleaning lady, I would have died. I was unable to get out of bed and no one knew where I was. For over a week the maid fed me broth and gave me water. I had such a high fever that I was either unconscious or totally unaware of my condition. I was unable to make it to the outside toilet, so she changed my sheets and washed me. After my recovery I tried to pay her but she only accepted a small amount for the broth. Good people exist in this world and I was lucky to have one on my doorstep.

I found Asia and particularly Indonesia corrupt from top to bottom. I found it appalling that I had to "bribe" everyone to get anything done. A few times I had to pay "extra" to get a seat on a flight because, "your reservation was lost!"

Poverty was in my face every day and yet people seemed to be happy. Smiles were everywhere. Children would gather around me wanting to practice their English, smiling and laughing all the while. It gave me an appreciation of how much I had compared to so many others. I was reborn in my new assignment. I learned things about myself that I didn't know and seemed to be getting back in touch with my soul.

My divorce came through while I was in Singapore and I swore I would never marry again. I was starting to enjoy being free and not feel guilty about my shortcomings.

Elroy Ackerman (Ack) and Don Naugle returned home from Vietnam and were in the first wave laid off. I have no idea what happened to them. Jack Norton and I kept in contact for years after our return from Vietnam. Jack was fortunate to get one military assignment after another. For more than five years during the 70s, Jack was under a military contract to the Thai Air Force on the OV-10 program. I saw Jack and his wife Barbie in Thailand on a regular basis.

I had civilian/commercial customers in Thailand and Jack and I would always spend time together and talk about the good old days. Barbie had a distinctive Bostonian accent and was quite the Asian shopper. Jack desperately tried to transfer from the military to a civilian program. He was never successful and continued with overseas military contracts until his retirement. I lost track of Jack during the next ten years. Gary McIntire is retired and settled on a farm in Ohio. We continue to have a strong bonding friendship.

After my assignment in Singapore was complete, I was transferred to Brisbane, Australia. I arrived on June 1st 1981 and I met Susan in the first week. She had two children (Peta 12 and Christian 10) by a previous marriage. It was suggested by a "friend of a friend" that I contact her in Brisbane on arrival for a "good home cooked meal". Susan was special and I knew it from the beginning. She was unlike any woman I had ever met. She was a nurse, intelligent, caring, attractive and also a fantastic cook and I fell in love with her! We were married on Nov 18th 1981.

I thought I would have a second chance to raise children and do it right this time, but initially I had a difficult relationship with Christian. At ten years old, Christian didn't want me in his family, which was understandable. All four of us had an adjustment period and went through some tough times, but everyone learned from each other. Now, I couldn't ask for a better relationship with Christian or Peta. I love them both like they were my own children. Looking back at almost 25 years of marriage, I can say that Susan and I are very happy. She has been very good for me and I think I've been good for her. I wouldn't give her up for anything and feel that, even with all my baggage, I have found a place in her heart.

Peta is a clinical nurse specializing in eating disorders. She is intelligent, witty and has a great personality. Peta is married to Neil, an Englishman (now Australian), and they have a beautiful baby boy, Callahan "Cal."

Christian at 30 plus years shares my love of traveling. He traveled all over Europe as a backpacker for a couple of years and loves the outdoors. Christian is a warm hearted, caring person talented in the visual arts. He works as an assistant art director, but I suspect that he would rather be working to save the world's environment.

Shortly after I arrived for my assignment in Brisbane I discovered that my son Doug was drug-dependant. His sister, Donna, had introduced him to drugs when he was 13 years old. I felt powerless to help him. Doug and his first wife, also an addict, had four children (Rachel, Christine, Nicole and Jessica); but the children were taken away by the state of Arizona and adopted by an anonymous couple. After years of battle, Doug finally freed himself of drugs, married Denelle and had a son Douglas Jr. Together with her two children

(Sunrise and Travis) they form a strong family unit. They own a carpet cleaning franchise, which keeps the bills paid.

I am very proud of Doug; he is a courageous individual and a loving father who was heart broken over the loss of his daughters. Our whole extended family are thrilled that contact with the girls has been re-established after more than fifteen years. Sadly, Doug's past caught up with him when he tested positive for the Hepatitis C virus. He was on a trial medication for a year and I am happy to say, the virus is dormant at this time.

I have no idea how much Denise suffered from her exposure to a separated family or the death of her sister. She never seemed to be unhappy and appeared well adjusted, so I was very surprised when she became pregnant at 15. She married the young man but that only lasted a short while. Denise has two children (Meagan, from her first marriage and Spencer from her second). Denise is currently happy in her third marriage and has her own lucrative real estate agency in Phoenix.

I can only assume that the depression that I developed during and after Vietnam had a huge negative impact on the stability of my children's lives. On the other hand, perhaps it gave them the strength to be able to recognize when they had a problem and work through it. I like to think this is the positive that came from the negative. The children had to work things out from a young age with little guidance from their mother or me. As adults they both know that I love them unconditionally and am always there for advice and support should the need arise. I have learned to accept that they make their own choices and I couldn't ask for two better, more understanding and caring children.

Doris has remarried. The last I heard, Judy was single after her fifth divorce. When I heard this news, I didn't feel so bad about not being able to make our marriage work.

In Dad's final years we became close friends. During the summer, we would sit on his porch, in his broken lawn chairs and he would ask me questions about my life. He was living below the poverty line in a run down shack in the country hills of Pennsylvania. Rusted out junk cars were scattered in the uncut grass around the shack. There was often a mongrel dog at his feet. When flies circled the dog's head to bite him, the dog adeptly made a quick, precision "snap", and the fly was in his mouth. In between Dad's questions he assisted the dog by killing an equal number of flies with his brightly colored plastic swatter. The dog seldom missed and neither did Dad.

Through our talks, I could see a side of my father that I had never experienced before and it was reciprocal. Many things went unsaid. He never apologized for the mental anguish he caused. I tried to get him to express his feelings by telling him, "I'm sorry we didn't have a good relationship when I was a boy, but I forgive you for that." He just nodded his head and said thanks but he couldn't bring himself to say that he was sorry or tell me that he loved me. Fortunately, I could see it in his face and accepted that as an indication of his respect and love. My father died of "black-lung" on May 25, 1991, aged 72. At the time, he was with his second family -- his ex-mistress and later wife and their five children.

My mother is living in an "assisted living" home in Pittsburgh. She is in good health but suffering from dementia. It breaks my heart to see her in that condition. She has never lost faith in me.

At this point in my life, I've learned that life is full of gifts, if you know where to look. I've have had the opportunity to experience a host of events and adventures that are only dreamed of by many. Some of the best were becoming a private pilot, achieving intermediate hang glider pilot status, obtaining the rank of brown belt in Judo, qualifying as an advanced SCUBA diver with more than 600 dives world wide, and becoming a proficient Ocean Yachtsman.

I have been a motorcycle rider and enthusiast since I was 13. I've owned numerous types of motorcycles and when younger, loved dirt riding and hill climbs. I made a trip with my 1100cc Honda from Perth to Brisbane, covering over 5,000 miles. In my opinion, the most dangerous aspect of the trip was the wedge-tail eagles and other large birds, feeding from the fresh road kill of kangaroos. As I approached the carcass, the eagles would remain on it till the last few seconds before taking flight. On three occasions I took bird hits to my body and helmet and would have taken many more if the motorcycle fairing hadn't taken the impact. A car might pass every 15 to 30 minutes and had I been knocked down by a bird and crashed off the main road, there was little chance of being noticed in the bushes.

I've had a few other brushes with death during my adventures. One of them was when I had to make a forced landing in a plowed muddy field with my single engine Stensin, after the engine failed at 800 feet altitude. I walked away from it without any damage to the aircraft or myself. Years later, I had a hang gliding accident. I flew into the trees and the glider was almost a write off. However, I came out of it with only an injury to my right knee and perhaps, my pride.

I sailed a 32-foot trimaran that I bought from Jack Norton, from Thailand to Singapore in 1979. It was a bad time to so close to Vietnam amongst all the refugees (boat people). Thai pirates impersonating fishermen were everywhere on the high seas. Typically they would board a refugee boat, steal their gold, rape the women and in many cases kill everyone on board and sink the craft. While my partner and I were underway one calm night on the South China Sea, six or seven Thai pirates dressed in sarongs wrapped around their waists and armed with automatic weapons, boarded my yacht. I didn't attempt to resist the pirates. I had been advised to be passive if boarded, as this would increase the chance of survival. I was also warned, not to take anything valuable on the yacht. The rationale was, if the pirates stole anything of value, they would most likely kill us and sink the boat so no evidence would remain. I was glad I followed the advice. The pirates scoured the yacht, didn't steal anything and left us unscathed.

Years later on a night-dive in Papua New Guinea in stormy seas, while on the bottom at 50 feet, I was shocked (but fortunate) to see a disturbance in the sand. The rough sea, aided by the strong current, had pulled the anchor out allowing it to drag along the bottom. I quickly swam over and grabbed the anchor as it swung free. I hung on for grim death while it was winched onto the boat, and when it reached the surface the Captain was very surprised to see me dangling. I could easily have been left behind.

I know now that in my early years, I made more wrong decisions about my personal life than right ones. But today, I am satisfied to wake up in the morning and know that there are people who love me, no matter what my past has been. I still have one major regret -- that I was not present as a devoted father for Donna, Doug and Denise when they really needed me. I would have liked to spend more time with them in their adolescence, to share in their development. But I keep asking myself, would it have made any difference? Maybe, maybe not. I tried in the best way I could, under the circumstances, after the divorce from their mother, to give them support not only financially, but also with love and understanding. It's been a bumpy road for all of us.

Hopefully when I'm just a memory, it can be said: "His life wasn't a total loss. He loved his wife Susan, all of his children and had some good influence on their lives". What more can I ask?

In my career I have been very fortunate that I have been able to play a small part in the advancement of turbo prop and fanjet powered aircraft. In May 1976, I was part of the Garrett team that broke the world record with a Lear 36, registration number N220Y. The TFE731 engine powered Lear, under the command of golfer Arnold Palmer was flown around the world in a record 57 hours 25 minutes and 42 seconds. One flight leg was from Boston to Paris. I was waiting for the Lear to arrive in Boston to debrief Arnie on any in-flight engine problems. Before the Lear departed for Paris I performed a preflight on both engines. I was absolutely thrilled to take part in this historic event.

Susan and I live in Brisbane, Australia and have no plans to move elsewhere. I retired from Garrett (now Honeywell) after 25 years of service and presently work part time as a consultant in the aircraft industry looking after; you guessed it, Garrett Engines. For me, getting into the field of aviation was very difficult, but getting out at any age is nigh on impossible!

"TWO HUNDRED YANKEE" Record setting flight around the world.
Top: Briefing (left to right) Captain: Arnold Palmer, Richard Ingelido, Flight Observer: Robert J. Sterling
Bottom Photo: Richard Ingelido performing a "pre-flight" on 200Y before departure from Boston to Paris

178

Looking Back on the Vietnam Conflict

Men and women on both sides fought for different reasons or beliefs. Families on both sides lost love ones in their struggle. The conflict in Vietnam was similar, yet different than any other war. There was extensive loss with nothing much gained. Blood was spilled and hopes were dashed as South Vietnam fought for their freedom against communism and the invasion of their country. *Initially* I was shattered to see the U.S. pullout and abandon all the desperate and loyal people into the hands of the North Vietnamese, but on the other hand the U.S. had been there too long and far to many lives (estimated two to three million) were lost due to politics then greed. Pleasant dreams were turned to nightmares.

In the end, North and South Vietnam became one country and, now ironically, communism is no longer a threat to the United States. Little did the free world know that communism would die a natural death. Evolution transformed it into an awkward style of free enterprise in a non-threatening way. Three and a half decades after the war, the Vietnamese are still suffering the debilitating side effects of the conflict in one way or another. I learned that the Vietnamese as a race of people are kind very forgiving and love their children as much or more than people in the Western World. There are good and bad in every race but overall I have a high regard for the Vietnamese.

Yet I'm not sure that we went into Vietnam for all the right reasons. Most Americans believed in the "domino effect theory" and that the spread of communism must be stopped, but were we told the whole truth? Since the war, I learned about the huge oil reserves in the delta area of Vietnam. I was discretely informed by a reliable source from Mobil Oil in Singapore that during the war Mobil found large deposits of oil that were to remain capped until the U.S. won the war. As we know, the U.S. didn't win, but before the withdrawal Mobil secured the wells and kept the location a secret. They planned at sometime in the future, to negotiate with the Vietnamese to return and open the capped wells. The negotiations failed but it appears that Mobil and the U.S. are still desperate to get back into Vietnam.

What I learned about others and myself:

In many ways, this book is not about the war in Vietnam. Instead, it recounts how I explored what it takes to survive and move on, despite the attacks of the internal demons of post-traumatic stress and minefields left by those who claim to care. Against the background of a country going through similar struggles, I finally discovered the path to a painful peace.

In my life I have learned to trust and love myself and accept my shortcomings. I had to get to know myself, and learn what I wanted before I could share happiness with someone else again. I find it very difficult to summarize what I have learned from my experiences. I do know that every day is a bonus and should be used to do something to help yourself and your fellow man. Things in my life that are learned might not apply to others. I sincerely believe that whatever negatives you experience in your life can be turned to positives and, like energy, experience cannot be created or destroyed therefore I strongly believe that "For every action there is an opposite and equal reaction". The challenge is always to find that positive energy or force and take advantage of it. It takes a lot of work, but sometimes the opportunity is just not available. Most people in the world are unfortunate enough to live in a country that will never provide an opportunity to escape from poverty. For those, it is only survival from day to day.

When I look back, my life has consisted of peaks and troughs with an overall steady improvement in all aspects. Without my spinal injury I would never have been able to further my education and experience the enriched life that I have lived. I know now that I could lose everything I own and still have the things that count the most in life, -my health and my loved ones.

Writing this book has been painful yet very therapeutic for me, but reflection leaves me with little faith in my fellow man. I see greed, self-indulgence, religion and values, and aggression keeping the world on its' knees. Most governments are burdened with these deficiencies as well. Are we born with one or all of these traits or do we learn them? Perhaps these things are normal but when carried to callous extremes there is enormous fall-out.

I have learned not I trust, or count on, some higher power to fix my problems or the world's. If there is a "forgiving God", he will forgive me for not believing. I don't believe that any God would allow the suffering of "his children" that exists in the world. So it appears to me that, "humanity is on it's own to combat the suffering of the world".

Miscellaneous Information
States in the U.S. I visited: 49 States but never North Dakota.
States I Lived in: Pennsylvania, Ohio, Michigan, South Carolina, New Jersey, Maryland, New York, Connecticut, Kansas, Arizona, and California.
Countries or Territories I visited: USA, Mexico, Nicaragua, Canada, Cuba, Bermuda, Greenland, England, Denmark, France, Germany, Spain, Portugal, Switzerland, Italy, Israel, Turkey, Greece, Egypt, Nepal, India, Sri Lanka, Thailand, Laos, Vietnam, China, Japan, Okinawa, Taiwan, Philippines, East and West Malaysia, Singapore, Indonesia, Solomon Islands, Pupa New Guinea, New Caledonia, Nauru, Guam, Fiji, Kiribati, Tuvalu, Tonga, Tahiti, New Zealand (North and South) and Australia where I gained Citizenship.

Glossary of Terms

AiResearch: A company founded by Cliff Garrett, providing the latest technological advancements in aircraft. Over the years, the company went public followed by a few takeovers. Some of the names that followed were Garrett Corporation, Signal Oil, Allied Signal and currently Honeywell.

AK-47: The AK-47 was the basic infantry weapon of the North Vietnamese Army and Viet Cong. Originally manufactured by the Russians; China copied and mass-produced the majority of the AK's. The AK-47 was actually a better performing and more reliable weapon than the M-16 provided to the U.S. military.

Angry Two: Nickname for VMO-2 flight group located at "Marble" Mountain Air Field (MMAF).

AO: Arial Observer. A person assigned to fly for aerial observation. Usually enlisted from infantry, artillery, or intelligence billets.

AO: Area of Operations also.

AOG: Aircraft On Ground. The expression used for an aircraft grounded for any maintenance condition that would cause the aircraft to be unworthy to fly.

Ba Moi-Ba: "33" Vietnamese Beer, Known as "tiger piss."

boom boom: "Quickie" with a prostitute, usually cost $3 to $5.

Bronco: See OV-10.

C-130 Hercules: A High wing cargo aircraft built by Lockheed. Powered by four Allison T-56 turboprop engines.

cabbage patch: A group of thatched huts just outside MMAF where Vietnamese girls worked as prostitutes.

caca dau: Vietnamese for "I'll kill you."

canopy: Plexiglas/clear plastic "bubble" covering for the cockpit.

cargo bay: Area in a vessel to store luggage or goods for shipment.

CER shop: Complete Engine Repair shop. The T76 engine could be repaired in this shop including the replacement of the compressor / turbine "rotor" as an assembly.

Charlie: Viet Cong or VC.

Charlie's Navy: Local Vietnamese fisherman in their fishing boats at sea.

Charlie Ridge: A prominent ridge of mountainous terrain approximately 20 miles south west of Da Nang that afforded the Viet Cong a route from Laos into the Da Nang area. It was the site of many Marine operations aimed at disrupting Charlie's movement of men and supplies.

cherry: New troop in Vietnam. Note FNG.

CH-46 Sea Knight: a medium lift assault helicopter.
   Manufacturer: Boeing Vertol Company
   Mission: The mission of the CH-46 Sea Knight helicopter in a Marine Medium Helicopter (HMM) is transport of combat troops, supplies, and equipment during amphibious and subsequent onshore operations. Troop assault is the primary function and the movement of supplies and equipment is secondary.
CH-47 Chinook: Boeing Vertol helicopter, known as the "shithook" due to it's lifting capability. Powered by two T55 Lycoming free power turbine engines.
CH-53 Sea Stallion: The Sikorsky CH-53 is a medium lift helicopter designed to transport personnel, supplies and equipment in support of amphibious and/or shore operations. Powered with General Electric T64 free power turbine engines.
chopper: Any helicopter.
collective: A flight control "stick" in the cockpit of a helicopter on the left side of the pilot, that when lifted, the blades / rotors increase blade angle and lift the helicopter in a vertical position.
crew chief: Flight crew member on a helicopter that maintained the aircraft.
crotch: Marine infantry, known as being "in the crotch."
CYA: Cover your ass; as in make sure you're not in an exposed position.
cyclic: A control "stick" in the cockpit of a helicopter between the pilots legs, that when moved forward or aft, left or right will change the main rotor blade angle, to allow the helicopter to move in the same direction that the cyclic stick is moved.
cyclo: A pedal powered "three wheeled vehicle" used as a cheap taxi service. The driver peddled from the back at the rear wheel and the rider sits (exposed) in the front.
cyclo girl: A term that a virtuous Vietnamese girl would use to describe a prostitute. In other words, "she would take anyone for a ride."
Da Nang Main: Da Nang main airport, in I Corp.
decouple: The loss of drive between the engine power section and the propeller. Due to the loss of propeller load the power section is free to over speed to a point of a turbine disc (uncontained) failure.
di di: Vietnamese phrase; "go quickly.
dinky dau: Vietnamese phrase for "you're crazy."
DMZ: Demilitarized zone or cease fire line established on 22 July 1954, by the United Nations. At that time French Indo China was partitioned into two countries (North and South Vietnam).
dong: Vietnamese currency known as Piasters or "P"
dung lai: Vietnamese for "stop" or "halt."
EM: Enlisted Men - men below the rank of sergeant

182

F-4 Phantom: The F-4 Phantom, McDonnell, aircraft is a twin-engine, all-weather, fighter-bomber. The Phantom was first used by the U.S. Navy as an interceptor but also used to fly as a ground-support bomber for the U.S. Marine Corps. The aircraft performed three tactical air roles in Vietnam: Air superiority, interdiction and close air support. McDonnell designed the F-4 and it was one of the greatest fighters of the postwar-era.

FAC: Forward Air Controller, person or aircraft, usually flying at a low-level, slow airspeed, had the responsibility for calling in air strikes on enemy positions.

feathered engine: A loose term that actually means to feather the engine propeller. When the engine is shut down in flight, it is a method of reducing propeller drag by placing the propeller blades in line with the flight path.

FNG: Translated to "fucking new guy!"

free fire zone: A battle area or combat zone in which no restrictions are placed on the use of arms or explosives.

fubar: Short for "fucked up beyond all repair or recognition." Used to describe equipment, persons, or situations.

ga mug: Vietnamese for "thank you."

Garrett: Cliff Garrett the founder of AiResearch. The engines designed and manufactured by AiResearch were given his name, "Garrett Engines"

GI: Government infantry or government issue.

Gook: Derogatory term for an Asian person. See Slope (head).

grunt: Hard core combat marine. Also, "ground-pounder."

gung ho: Very committed and enthusiastic, as in a "gung ho Marine!"

Hai Van Pass: A treacherous pass through the mountains between Da Nang and Phu Bai.

Highway One: Main road running north and south from Saigon to Hanoi.

Ho Chi Minh Road Runners: "thong" type shoes, made by the Vietnamese, with the soles made of truck tires.

hooch: Hut or living quarters large enough to sleep 5 to 6 men comfortably.

I Corps: Northernmost military region in South Vietnam. The headquarters of I Corps was located in Da Nang. I Corps was one of four major military regions and administrative units of the South Vietnamese government.

I & I: Intoxication and Intercourse. Term used in lieu of R&R.

incoming: Receiving enemy rockets or mortar.

In Country: Vietnam (in Vietnam)

inop: Inoperative or not functioning.

leatherneck: A marine. In 1798 through 1880 the Marines wore a leather
    neckband for protection of the neck during sword combat.

lifer: Career military personnel often derogatory

LZ: Landing Zone

MACV: (mac-vee) Military Assistance Command, Vietnam

MAG: Marine Air Group - such as MAG-16 under the umbrella of the 1st
    Marine Air Wing.

mama san: Mature or older Vietnamese female, usually a mother.

mama san bike: "Step through" scooter motorcycle.

Marble Mountains: About eight miles south of Da Nang were five marble
    extrusions (mountains) rising directly from the sand adjacent to
    China Beach. They ranged in height from about 100 to about 500
    ft. There were a series of caves throughout the mountains that were
    used by Charlie for many subversive activities. The mountains in
    Vietnamese folklore are named water, metal, wood, fire and earth.

Marston matting: Named after the inventor (Marston). Otherwise known as
    PSP, it was a heavy gauge steel sheet. In a cross section, each sheet
    was in the shape of metal decking with punched lightening holes,
    interlocking slots and tabs to hold them together.

MAW: 1st Marine Air Wing or commonly called "The Wing."

medivac: Acronym for medical evacuation, almost always associated with
    evacuation of casualties by helicopter during or after a battle.

mess: Food or chow

MIA: Missing In Action

MMAF: "Marble" Mountain Air Field (Air Base)

MOS: Military Operation Specialties. Some of the Vietnam-era codes
    were: 6018: OV-10 mechanic
                 6023: T76 engine mechanic
                 7576: VMO pilot, OV-10

MPC: Military Payment Certificates. The MPC was used by the military instead of U.S. dollars in Vietnam. Example of a five cent MPC paper note is below:

Napalm: (BLU-32): A firebomb consisting of a thin skinned container of fuel gel. These 500 lb containers were finned which allowed for a more accurate and predictable trajectory. If the fins were removed, the canisters would tumble unpredictably after release from the aircraft that created a wider dispersion pattern for the napalm. Napalm was used as an incendiary type weapon.

NCO: Non Commissioned Officer

North American Aviation: The airframe manufacturer of the OV-10 along with various other military aircraft. The main factory was in Columbus, Ohio.

number one: Term used to describe the best.

number ten: Term used to describe the worst.

NVA: North Vietnamese Army

old salts: Military personnel that had years of experience in the service.

OV-10: See pages 11 and 189

over speed (engine): The engine compressor or turbine rotating group spins/rotates greater than it's design limitation.

papa san: An elderly Vietnamese man, usually a father.

185

pilot preflight: A "light" inspection of an aircraft by the pilot just prior to his departure.

pisser/s: Pissers (urinals) were strategically placed around the base. They consisted of a 55 gal steel drum perforated with holes and buried in the sand with the top slightly above ground level. A three sided, waist high corrugated steel barricade surrounded the buried drum, for limited privacy.

PSP: Perforated Steel Planking. See Marston matting.

pucker factor: Measurement of one's "fear factor" or how tight your ass tightened in a difficult or risky situation.

puff: Other wise known as "puff the magic dragon." Puff was a C-47 (military version of a DC-3) gunship with 3 mini 7.62mm mini gattling guns protruding from the open windows on the left hand side of the aircraft. Each mini gun was capable of firing 6,000 rounds a minute or all three guns could be used at the same time, firing a total of 18,000 rounds per minute.

PX: Post Exchange (BX: Base Exchange)

relief tube: A tube through the floor of an aircraft, with a funnel attached to the cabin end. Used to urinate into.

revetments: high walled protective barriers.

ROK: "Rock." Republic of Korea: Korean "hard core mercenary marines."

round eye: Slang term used by American troops to identify Non-Asians.

R&R: Rest and Recuperation or leave entitlement. (See I&I)

RVN: Republic of Vietnam Troops

sappers: North Vietnamese Army or VC suicide demolition commandos.

short: A term used to describe the days remaining before reassignment from active duty in Vietnam to the U.S. or another country post. It could also be used to describe how many days were remaining of the time before their final discharge of military service. "**Fuck it, I'm short!**" In other words, "I'm leaving here very soon and couldn't care less what's going on around me."

short timers calendar: A segmented, "color-in by number", picture that was filled in for each day in Vietnam. The last segment would be the last remaining day in country, completing the picture.

SHP: Shaft Horse Power

slick: Bell "Huey" helicopter without rocket pods or mounted guns.

slope (head): A derogatory term used to refer to any Asian (see Gook).

snafu: situation normal, all fucked up.

snoop "n" poop: Marine search and destroy offensive mission.

sortie: One aircraft making one take-off and landing to conduct a mission for which it was intended.

STOL: Short Take Off and Land

T76 Engine: Garrett Turbo Prop Engine. (See OV-10 for more detail)
A fixed shaft, two stage centrifugal compressor, three stage power turbine engine that produces 715 SHP.
Engine Rotation Speed: 41,730 rpm @ 100% (design speed)
Prop Speed: 2,000 rpm @ 100% engine speed.

tarmac: Hard surface, "black top" (gravel held together with tar). In most cases it was around taxi areas, around the flight line and hangars

tee tee: Vietnamese term for "a little bit"

TET (Tet): Literally, Tet Nguyen Dan means the first morning of the first day of the new period. Tet is the lunar New Year Festival and it is the most important Vietnamese holiday period.

un-contained failure: When an engine part fails and pieces of the failed part are not contained within the engine case.

up country: Referred to the northern most land mass of South Vietnam

VC / Cong: Viet Cong. Resistance fighters in South Vietnam assisting North Vietnam but not a part of the North Vietnam regular army.

VMO: Acronym for a "V" fixed wing, "M" Marine, "O" Observation type aircraft.

Yards: Moutaignard soldiers

OV-10 expanded details

The OV-10 (Bronco) is a rugged, maneuverable, twin-turboprop, multi-mission aircraft that served with the U.S. Air Force and Marine Corps in the Vietnam War. The U.S. Navy also used the OV-10. The Navy squadron VAL-4, "Black Ponies", flew them with success in Vietnam. Designed and built by the company North American in Columbus, Ohio, the OV-10 complemented the performance requirements between jets and helicopters. They were faster and more tactically versatile than helicopters, yet slower and more maneuverable than jets. The OV-10 utilized tactics not possible with either.

The OV-10D night observation system (NOS) featured a unique night observation and target marking system that included forward-looking infrared (FLIR) and laser designator/ranger. Initially designed and delivered with Garrett T76 turboprop engines with 715 shaft horsepower (SHP), later upgraded to 1040 SHP engines and fiberglass propellers.

North American Aviation initially submitted a proposal to the government to have the Pratt & Whitney PT-6 engine installed. The PT-6 had been around a few years already and was proving to be a reliable engine. The Garrett T76 engine on the other hand, was mostly a "paper" engine. In other words, it was not yet out of the experimental stage.

The government was interested in the 715 shaft horsepower Garrett engine for the OV-10 installation, as it was a fixed shaft power section. Therefore, the Garrett engine was much more responsive (in power) than the free power turbine of a PT-6. The T76 two stage centrifugal compressor was also much less susceptible to erosion or foreign object damage (FOD). The PT-6 had an axial stage compressor design and was very susceptible to erosion and FOD. Dirt and FOD was a major consideration. The Garrett engine was also lighter than the PT-6 and slightly higher in horsepower.

North American however, was adamant that they didn't want the Garrett engine on "their" airplane. In the end the U.S. contract was given to AiReseach/Garrett to supply the T76. To smooth the ruffled feathers of North American and spread the contracts around, the power management system installed on the T76 was designed and supplied by Hamilton Standard, a sister company of P&W. The Power Management Control (PMC) system was termed the PMC-5 and consisted of the Prop Governor (PG), Prop Pitch Control (PPC), Propeller, Beta Tube (supplies oil from PPC to the Prop) and Three "D" Cam Assembly (Linkage Control).

One of the design functions of the PMC-5 allowed the pilot to loiter the aircraft at greatly reduced cruise speeds. Instead of the normal 96% Prop Governor (PG) setting at cruise, the RPM could be reduced to 85% with the speed lever. If for any reason the pilot needed to make an expeditious application of power from loitering at 85%, he need only to move the Power Lever forward. This would increase the Prop Governor RPM to 100% along with the increase in fuel flow.

In military operations, the Bronco's outstanding capability to find and hit battlefield targets close to friendly troops made this aircraft effective against conventional and guerilla forces. Applications for which the Bronco was particularly suited include, intelligence observation platform, anti-guerrilla operations, helicopter escort, close air support, armed reconnaissance, and forward air control. In addition, it could be used for utility missions such as cargo "para drop", delivery of up to six paratroops, medical evacuation, smoke screening, and psychological warfare with leaflets and loudspeakers.

Ruggedness and simplicity of operation were emphasized in the design of the Bronco. The fuselage was mounted under the wing and provided tandem seating for pilot and observer. The canopy design afforded better visibility than that of most helicopters. Each crewman was equipped with an LW-3B ejection seat system, also designed and built at Columbus, which was capable of zero-speed, zero-altitude ejections. Armor protection, bullet-resistant windshield, and self-sealing fuel cells were provided for operations in a hostile environment. Twin engines, dual manual flight controls, and rugged and simple construction also contributed to survivability and safety.

The OV-10 was equipped with seven external store stations and four 7.62mm guns installed in the sponsons. A variety of conventional ordinance could be delivered in addition to 2,000 rounds of ammunition. The seven external store stations consisted of four sponsons / extensions, one centerline station, and two external wing station sponsons on each side. Sponson accessibility provided rapid loading of stores and ammunition. (Note "OV-10 / Line Drawing" for actual locations*). The wing stations could carry the LAU-7/A launcher for mounting either rocket packages or missiles. The centerline store station also had the capability of carrying either a 20mm gun pod or a 150-, 230-, or 300 gallon (568-, 871-, or 1136 liter) external fuel tank.

For operation in remote areas, the Bronco had specially designed rough field landing gear, that required no ground equipment for starting, and could be maintained with simple hand tools. In the event of an emergency, the Bronco could use high-octane or automotive fuel in place of jet fuel with only a slight degradation of power.

Later in peacetime operations, the aircraft became a high-performance STOL (Short Take Off and Land) utility vehicle. Removal of the armament sponsons and the back seat with its associated armor enabled a quick and simple conversion that permitted the carrying of 3,200 pounds (1,452 kilograms) of cargo in the aft fuselage.

Order Book/s by email: NotAboutWar@yahoo.com